W9-BTC-155

7SECRETS OF GREAT ENTREPRENEURIAL MASTERS

THE GEM POWER FORMULA
FOR LIFELONG SUCCESS

7SECRETS OF GREAT ENTREPRENEURIAL MASTERS

ALLEN E. FISHMAN

McGraw·Hill

New York   Chicago   San Francisco   Lisbon   London   Madrid   Mexico City
Milan   New Delhi   San Juan   Seoul   Singapore   Sydney   Toronto

The **McGraw·Hill** Companies

Copyright © 2006 by Allen E. Fishman. All rights reserved. Printed in the United States of America. Except as permitted under the United States Copyright Act of 1976, no part of this publication may be reproduced or distributed in any form or by any means, or stored in a database or retrieval system, without the prior written permission of the publisher.

1 2 3 4 5 6 7 8 9 0   DOC/DOC   0 9 8 7 6

ISBN 0-07-147071-9

The Alternative Board, Strategic Business Leadership (SBL), GEM Power, Pocket Vision, TABenos, and Tips from the Top are trademarks of TAB Boards International, Inc.

McGraw-Hill books are available at special quantity discounts to use as premiums and sales promotions, or for use in corporate training programs. For more information, please write to the Director of Special Sales, Professional Publishing, McGraw-Hill, Two Penn Plaza, New York, NY 10121-2298. Or contact your local bookstore.

 This book is printed on recycled, acid-free paper containing a minimum of 50% recycled, de-inked fiber.

Library of Congress Cataloging-in-Publication Data
Fishman, Allen E.
   Seven secrets of great entrepreneurial masters : the GEM power formula for lifelong success / by Allen E. Fishman.—1st ed.
      p. cm.
   Includes index.
   ISBN 0-07-147071-9 (alk. paper)
1. Vocational guidance.   2. Quality of work life.   3. Life skills.   4. Success—
Psychological aspects.   I. Title.
   HF5381.F484 2006
   650.1—dc22

                                                                  2006013617

To my mother, Esther, a woman who has a zest for life, a very special sense of humor, and a positive attitude like no one else I have ever met. She is an incredibly loving mother who always communicates her love to me both verbally and physically. There is no way to express how deeply appreciative I am for that love.

Contents

Foreword

Most people spend more time planning the details of a two-week vacation than they spend planning their lives. Allen Fishman is not one of those people. Allen has successfully balanced life and work while raising a family, overseeing various growing enterprises, and enjoying numerous outdoor recreational activities.

He now shares his private success formula in this exciting, informative book, the *Seven Secrets of Great Entrepreneurial Masters*, so that others may share the same happiness, fulfillment, and life balance he has achieved.

In the more than 15 years I have personally known Allen, I have found him to be a passionate, oft-times driven man in business, a loving father, and a doting grandfather. He is truly someone who "walks the talk" of what he has taught others over the years around the world. On these pages he now "gives back" what he has learned through personal experience and by dealing with thousands of business owners through the peer advisory organization he founded in 1990, TAB Boards International.

Having applied the *Secrets of Great Entrepreneurial Masters* in my own life, I have experienced firsthand the joys, triumphs, and sense of accomplishment these exercises and practices can afford anyone, whether a current business owner, seasoned executive, or aspiring entrepreneur.

You are to be congratulated for reading this book and applying its wisdom. You are about to reap huge rewards for doing so. Contained herein are the keys for you to unlock the doors of lasting success, both in your business and in your personal life.

Greg Walker
President
PCS Systems, Inc.

Preface

As a small-business owner, my personal life is inextricably inter-twined with my business life. Every major decision I make has potential impact on all aspects of my life, not just my business life. Both my personal and business lives are responsible for creating the dynamics that have given me the ability to be successful and happy in my role of entrepreneur. I have created a situation in which I work only when I want to, and only with those whom I choose.

In 1990, I identified what seemed to me to be the greatest need of small-business owners: the need for peer advice from fellow business owners and coaching from experienced professionals who were armed with a process to achieve greater personal and business success. The recognition of this need was the inspiration that led me to start a new business, TAB Boards International, Inc., which operates under the name The Alternative Board and is commonly referred to by the acronym TAB. I feel a great sense of pride that TAB has grown into the largest peer advisory and business owner coaching franchise system in the world.

My primary home is in the Aspen area. TAB's international head-quarters are located in Denver. Most of the time I am a long-distance CEO who uses the phone or e-mail for business matters. I can hang up the phone, or turn off the computer, and walk outside to enjoy the day by hiking or biking or by catching a chairlift up the slopes to go skiing.

My role in TAB fulfills a personal need, but it also allows me the time to enjoy the equally important, nonwork facets of my life. I thrive on being a catalyst for the success of TAB by coming up with new ideas and strategies. I do what I am good at in my work for TAB—and I do it on my own terms. What more could a business owner ask for?

I am living the Personal Vision I dreamed of when I started The Alternative Board. TAB is making a difference in the lives of thousands of business owners around the world. I work with people I like and respect, and I do the things I enjoy in an environment of my choosing. I hold the position of CEO. My son-in-law, Jason Zickerman, has the position of president and COO, and I have the honor of mentoring him.

My good fortune did not happen by chance. The foundation for it was set while I was quite young. My belief in dreams, and what my father taught me about achieving my dreams, has played a part in every step of my professional life and is one of the underlying principles of the Seven Secrets presented in this book.

My father enlightened me as to the importance of establishing a connection between work and personal life. He viewed business as being an important part of life, but still only part of the life that he wanted to be living. I clearly remember his standing over me as I played the piano one night and telling me that I was blessed with ability and to set my dreams high so that I did not waste that ability. He taught me to plan for the future and how to think through all the possibilities a given situation had to offer before taking action.

My father believed that winners put themselves in control of their own futures instead of just reacting to situations or being subjected to the whims of others. He ingrained in me the importance of not overreacting to the actions of others, and he encouraged me to continually define and redefine my dreams while going after them. I was repeatedly told that patience, planning, and innovation were the needed ingredients for bringing my dreams to life.

Like most kids, I did not absorb the repeated messages from my father right away. Until my last year of high school, my relationship with academics could best be described as daydreaming in class, having no regard for homework assignments, and poor attendance. Enlightenment, however, did eventually kick in. I was fortunate that my first-year grades allowed me to gain an undergraduate academic scholarship. I graduated magna cum laude from Saint Louis University, which, along with my LSAT scores, gained me a full scholarship to law school. After receiving my JD from law school in 1966, I began my professional career practicing business law with a publicly owned company, the May Department Stores, which has since been acquired by the Federated Department Stores.

Only a few years after graduating from law school, I was managing the West Coast legal department of the May Department Stores Company. At age 27 I switched to the business side of the company and became the youngest (so I was told) nonfamily member to become a vice president of a subsidiary of May. I was on the corporate fast track, but even then there was no denying my desire to someday own my own business.

Eager to prepare for this entrepreneurial future, I left May to accept a position as a court-appointed receiver of a distribution company that was in default on its bank loan. Under my receivership, the distribution company developed and executed a strategic plan that allowed it to pay off its bank debt-in full-within 18 months.

After that valuable experience, I joined Tipton Centers, Inc., a privately owned, St. Louis-based, consumer-electronics retail and service company. The owner of Tipton, Syl Kaplan, had a dream of growing Tipton from four small stores in the St. Louis area into a major regional presence. He offered to sell me part ownership of the company as incentive to join Tipton. I saw Tipton as having the potential for outstanding success and jumped at the opportunity.

Being part owner, president, and COO of Tipton was an extremely exciting time. Each year was a record-breaking year. Tipton became a NASDAQ publicly traded company, and in 1987 it was sold to the industry's international leader. I was 45 years old when Tipton was sold. I recognized an opportunity to realize a dream and moved to the Aspen, Colorado, area in order to enjoy a semiretirement.

Although I withdrew from the day-to-day process of running a business, I didn't completely abandon the business world. I accepted speaking engagements before national and international business organizations that were interested in my views on the "GEM Power Formula for Lifelong Success."

I accepted an invitation from the *St. Louis Post-Dispatch* to write a column that shared my insights on entrepreneurial success. I called it *Business Insights*, and it became a nationally syndicated, weekly column distributed by Tribune Media Services. While writing the column, I interviewed hundreds of entrepreneurs regarding the processes, techniques, and tools responsible for their business success. I found the experience fascinating.

Barbra Streisand was once asked about happiness on a TV talk show. She answered that happiness was a difficult concept that she did not know much about. She added, "I'll settle for success." Similarly, many of the successful entrepreneurs I interviewed seemed to be settling for only success—not happiness. Interestingly, many of these successful entrepreneurs appeared to not be particularly happy outside of their business life. For them, happiness was an elusive concept.

In contrast to this, my observation of other successful business owners was that they were living happy lives. I refer to these business owners, who have achieved both a high level of personal happiness and success in their lives and businesses, as "Great Entrepreneurial Masters," or "GEMs." They are "Masters" because of their skill and proficiency at creating success and happiness. This book reveals Seven of the Secrets behind their varied and overwhelming successes.

Repeatedly, I found similarities between the methods that GEMs had used to create their successful personal and business lives and the methods I had used to achieve the same. I documented these methods, and they became the foundation of the Seven Secrets for success and happiness that I share in this book.

My regular contact, over many years, with a large number of TAB members put me in the position of being able to draw off the experiences of TAB Board members to help refine the Secrets. This contact provided me with unique insights to the Secrets—insights that are much different from those that a consultant would have. These TAB members include those who are still members of the first TAB Board formed, which I continue to facilitate.

The methodology of the Secrets was then modified as a result of practical use by TAB business owners around the world. This formula has since become an important tool to the success of thousands of TAB members.

You might be wondering why I have taken the time to write this book. During one of the first meetings to discuss the outline of this book, my daughter Lynette asked me this same question. My answer to her included a story about a famous horse whisperer of the early 1900s. He was so proud of his gift that he refused to share his knowledge with anyone—even his children—perhaps because he did not want to lose his fame for being able to calm the wildest of horses. Sadly, when he died, his knowledge went with him. As I told my daughter, I want to share the knowledge of those who have succeeded, as I have, as entrepreneurs because this knowledge has the potential to positively change the lives of others. Business owners, managers, and people in other walks of life can apply the *Secrets of Great Entrepreneurial Masters* to their own lives in order to achieve their own dreams.

Since moving my primary residence to the Aspen, Colorado, area in 1987, I have lived my dream life. I combine my passion for business with my passion for skiing, hiking, biking, horseback riding, and playing in some of the most beautiful surroundings that North America has to offer. When I feel the urge to travel, I go to the places I want to visit. I've been married to the same wonderful woman since I was 20 years old, and I am fortunate to be able to enjoy spending a great deal of time with my children, grandchildren, son-in-law, and other family members. My dogs and horses bring me a great deal of pleasure.

I'm a lucky guy. I am living my dreams with the help of the same belief system that is presented in this book. You can too. Let's get started on the road to your success.

Enjoy the trip.

Allen E. Fishman

Acknowledgments

W hen I was very young, my father told me, "When drinking the water, always remember the one who dug the well." Daily, I am grateful for the well Herman Fishman dug and for the water I drank from it. So much of my father's wisdom concerning business and life, which I have attempted to share in this book, resonates within me.

I would also like to gratefully acknowledge the many other individuals who helped me with this book, especially Lyn Adler. Her editing of the material has resulted in making the book more enjoyable to read. She took on the role of challenging me and recommending changes that fleshed out my stories. There were many times she coerced me to keep working when I wanted to cut our work sessions short to do something recreational. She was patient with my calls to dictate my ideas; calls that came from unusual locations like the tops of mountains while I was skiing or on the trails while riding my bike. Because of my unstructured time for working on the book, we communicated and worked on the book at hours that go beyond what most people consider normal work hours. Lyn is extremely unique and has made writing this book a wonderful experience.

My daughters, Lynette and Michele, had enormous impact on how the book took form through their two very diverse views. When my daughter Michele saw the first draft of this book, she told me that I should either relate my personal experiences for getting what I want out of life or tear up the draft. Innately, I knew she was right, but at the time I was not ready to write so openly. It was only after shelving the manuscript for a while that I was able to start working on it again using the approach that she so wisely demanded.

My other daughter, Lynette, was also involved during the early stages of the book. Her probing questions and advice impacted greatly on the development of the book. I have also been able to discuss ideas with her concerning the manuscript throughout the process.

My son-in-law, Jason Zickerman, who is president and chief operating officer of The Alternative Board, has been the moving force behind making the processes and techniques contained in this book an integral part of the way that TAB members live their lives and run their businesses. My experience with Jason has been, and continues to be, one that most fathers-in-law dream of but never get to experience. Family businesses are special. Sharing the joy with someone you love, as I love Jason, is a reward that goes far beyond the material benefits of the business. Thank you, Jason, for your belief in this book and for your continuous encouragement to devote the time needed to bring it to life.

Thanks to the thousands of TAB business-owner members around the world who use the processes and tools contained in this book to assist them in more thoroughly enjoying the present while planning for a future that leads to the fulfillment of their dreams. Many of these TAB members have shared their experiences with TAB, and I have used many of those experiences in this book. I have used the actual names of business owners only where I have been granted permission to do so. In paying respect to confidentiality, I have, in many cases, avoided using the true names of the people or the companies involved in the stories and examples provided in the book. I have in some instances changed some facts to ensure further confidentiality.

David Halpern, chief innovative officer of The Alternative Board, has brought a level of enthusiasm and energy in spreading the TAB "word" of which few would be capable. David's creative ideas and innovations have helped numerous business owners make the leap from their previous level of success to ultimately reaching the success they desired.

Thanks to Greg Walker who has trained so many TAB facilitator-coaches in different communities and countries to use the processes and techniques that are revealed in this book. Greg is one of the most naturally talented business professionals I have ever met. He has been especially helpful in giving suggestions and advice that appear throughout this book.

I appreciate the efforts of TAB Vice President Cheryl Swanson for taking the time to read the manuscript and giving me ideas for making the book more valuable to readers.

My regrets for the loss this year of Syl Kaplan, with whom I worked for many years and with whom I shared the experience and thrill of taking a company public. What a learning experience.

To my friends Ken Gutner and Barry Kash, thanks for the good times and for all our social-business conversations.

My deepest thanks go to TAB facilitator-coaches Otis Brinkley, Ray Brun, Doug Cash, Darrell Crawford, Carol Crawford, Steve Davies, John Dini, Barba Hickman, Oswald Viva, Alan Wallach, Chris White, and Carlos Zubillaga. They shared advice and stories based on their experiences using the material in this book to help their TAB members define and achieve their personal and business success. Their collective input has been enormously supportive in shaping this book.

A deep appreciation goes out to my business friends in the Aspen, Colorado, area who, while riding together up ski lifts, biking, hiking, and otherwise enjoying the blessings of living in such a wonderful place, have shared with me the factors behind their own successes. These men and women are among the most successful business owners in the world, and they are also among the most interesting.

Last, but not least, I want to thank my agent, Ron Goldfarb, for his invaluable advice on developing the proposal for this book.

INTRODUCTION

Are you ready to take control of—and get what you want from—your personal and business life? Whatever your business or age, if you are ready to take a closer look at your "authentic self" and assume full responsibility for living your life and leading your business, then the Seven Secrets of Great Entrepreneurial Masters (GEMs) will help you find the life you seek. If you are ready to start making conscious, strategic decisions that will lead to the enhanced enjoyment of both your personal and business lives, and if you are ready to attain your dreams, then the Seven Secrets of GEMs is a necessity.

The search for fulfillment and happiness in life is as individualistic as the one who is doing the seeking. Many people are searching for deeper meaning from life, but what exactly does that mean? What makes a life more fulfilling? Fulfillment is surely more than what modern Western culture implies: money, status, a new car, or even tremendous business success. Granted, these are all things that bring pleasure, but are they all that there is?

The Seven Secrets are a tested and proven approach that will enable you to create a clear definition of what fulfillment means to you—your Personal Vision of Success—and then will show you how to turn that vision into a reality. The Secrets help you map out what you desire from your personal life and your work life and then show you how to merge both to create the fulfilling life you desire.

Capturing the Essence of the Secrets

My early semiretirement to the Aspen, Colorado, area placed me in the midst of many others, who, like me, are Great Entrepreneurial Masters (GEMs)—those who have attained a level of happiness and success most people only dream about. While hiking the peaks and riding the ski lifts with this group of my peers, I came to realize that despite our different backgrounds, educations, and career paths, we had all applied most of the same basic elements to create our varied but substantial successes. I captured the essence of these shared elements and developed a formal process for using them—the Seven Secrets of Great Entrepreneurial Masters.

When I refer to entrepreneurs, I do not limit the term to include only those who are the founders or organizers of a business venture. My definition of entrepreneur refers to the person who has the final power in a business, the one who directs the company, and, of course, the one who takes the commercial risks relating to the ownership of the company.

The Secrets Will Work for Everyone

I have met a large number of nonbusiness owners who have found great benefit in applying the Seven Secrets to their personal and work lives. Most of them learned the basics of the Secrets by attending a talk with a business owner or by witnessing their boss apply the Seven Secrets. Anyone can successfully use most aspects of the Seven Secrets to achieve his or her dreams of success and happiness.

The Seven Secrets will work for anyone, from any walk of life, who wants greater personal and work success. The dreams of nonentrepreneurs may be different from those of entrepreneurs, but their dreams are every bit as attainable using the Seven Secrets of GEMs. As one GEM Power user stated, "Thanks to the Secrets of GEMs, my personal and work worlds meld together to satisfy the dreams I envisioned when I first looked into the future. The Secrets have changed my life."

The Alternative Board

In 1990 I founded TAB Boards International, Inc. Today, TAB operates the world's largest franchise system that provides peer advisory board and coaching services to entrepreneurs. TAB peer boards and TAB coaches provide owners of small to medium-sized businesses an opportunity to get essential personal and business advice from peers who know what life at the top is all about. I incorporated the Seven Secrets contained in this book into the coaching methods used today by TAB facilitator-coaches. The Secrets have helped the thousands of entrepreneurs located throughout the world who make up the TAB community to become GEMs.

Focusing with Written Statements

The Seven Secrets enable business owners, and those from all walks of life, to move from their existing level of success to the level of GEMs by showing them how to put their dreams for the future, a self-analysis, and their Personal Plans down on paper in short, concisely written statements. The first three chapters of this book provide helpful techniques, questions, and real-life examples to assist you in creating your written statements.

At The Alternative Board, we really stress the importance of putting things into writing. Writing is a process that helps you clarify your ideas. Kevin Armstrong, a TAB facilitator-coach in Vancouver, British Columbia, tells his members that written statements are essential and, therefore, "if it isn't written down, it doesn't exist."

You Are the Catalyst for Your Success

In order to achieve your dreams, you must run both your life and your business strategically. GEMs are masters at controlling their life and their work. They know this control is not a luxury—it's an essential factor in maximizing their success.

All too often, small-business owners who are not GEMs spend most of their time putting out day-to-day fires that are disguised as real or perceived business crises. Due to this role of "firefighter," the small-business owner often envisions great ideas but rarely gets around to making these ideas happen.

You can't reach your personal dreams without taking charge of your life. The Seven Secrets empower you with the ability to develop plans that are simple to follow, and they provide you with a framework on which to focus your energy.

Business owners are in control of what they do in their business. They control when they work, with whom they work, and the amount of money they take out from the earnings of the company. But even if you are not a business owner and do not possess the same absolute control over these factors, you do have enough control to use the Seven Secrets to change your life. Your success in life and the fulfillment you feel from your work will increase dramatically by applying the Secrets to your life.

Creating a Road Map to Success

The success of an entrepreneur's business is an important factor in creating personal happiness. However, if the business owner is miserable in what he or she does within the business and has no time to enjoy the nonbusiness aspects of life, he or she will not be able to find true personal happiness.

We all have unique situations and factors in our lives. The Seven Secrets initiate a personalized introspection that leads you in creating a road map that clearly outlines how to make the most of your personal situation in order to get the things you desire from life.

One of the key elements to success is realizing what is essential—not merely marginal—to living a happy life. The Seven Secrets will show you how to separate the wheat from the chaff in order to get what you want out of life. They will guide you through the introspection, planning, and actions needed to identify and achieve the dreams that make up your Personal Vision of success and happiness.

Don't think that the Seven Secrets are only about sacrifice and planning for the future. In addition to strategically planning for the future, the Seven Secrets will also show you how to appreciate and enjoy the present.

GEMs are masters at integrating everything they do as business owners and everything they do in their personal lives to bring about their Personal Vision of happiness. There are millions of non-GEM entrepreneurs who are successful in their work but who cannot find happiness. In part, this situation exists because they are not honest with themselves about the factors responsible for their unhappiness.

Far too many business owners

- Feel life is out of balance
- Can't find time to enjoy life
- Work more hours than they would like
- Don't enjoy doing what they do at work
- Feel alone
- Suffer from an absence of personal accountability
- Wish they could make more money
- Feel life is more stressful than they would like

Thousands have used the Seven Secrets of GEMs to eliminate every one of the problems listed above. This is a process I have personally used and a process in which I have utter faith that it will work for everyone who uses it.

Most people work hard to succeed, but the right formula for getting what they want eludes them. Too many simply go through the motions each day, accepting that "this" is the best they can achieve. Putting in outlandish hours and dealing with overwhelming stress and pervading loneliness along with a loss of joy in living are all commonly accepted by many people as a standard way of living. If your life is out of alignment with the direction you want to go, it is inevitable that you are not going to achieve your dreams.

The Seven Secrets are not limited to material success. My life is not limited to, or defined by, my material possessions. My life is a balance of my work, my personal interests, and the relationships I have with family and friends. The Seven Secrets are largely responsible for my being able to live a balanced life that most only envision—a life in which work success and personal happiness coalesce.

An Overview of the Seven Secrets of GEMs

- *The Secret of A Personal Vision.* The written, long-range dream of what you want out of life. GEMs include but do not limit their Personal Vision to factors relating to the level of financial and material success they desire. Your written Personal Vision will also identify the nonmaterial success factors you desire such as work role, balance between work and personal life, family and other relationships, mental and physical health, travel, retirement, psychic rewards, where you want to live, and any religious or spiritual aspects you want in your life. GEMs use their Personal Vision as both the foundation that supports their efforts and the target toward which they aim. To be effective, your Personal Vision must be realistically attainable. GEMs typically include in their Personal Vision Statement some ideas or information that they do not want to share with some or all of their family, friends, and employees. I refer to the parts of your Personal Vision that you choose not to share as your "Pocket Vision."

- *The Secret of A Look in the Mirror.* A written self-analysis that identifies your Strengths and Weaknesses and examines potential Opportunities and Threats as they pertain to your happiness and success. These four pieces of your personal mirror are collectively referred to as your "SWOT." The Secret of A Look in the Mirror is the framework GEMs use for achieving their dreams. You will learn how to identify personal factors such as passion, aptitude, and personality and learn how to use this information to build the plans you need to reach the destination of your dreams.

- *The Secret of The Personal Plan.* How to chart the course that will lead the way to your dreams. Discover how GEMs create written Personal Plans that help them achieve their Personal Vision. The Secret of the Personal Plan includes identifying the factors critical to your success, setting Goals to satisfy those Critical Success Factors, creating Strategies to achieve the Goals, and making Action Plans that will make your Strategies successful.
- *The Secret of Results-Driven Communications to Make It Happen.* The right communication techniques for igniting passion within those whose help you need to make your Personal Plans happen. GEMs use the Secret of Results-Driven Communications to bring their Personal Plans to life. This Secret starts by exploring the six methods GEMs use to build trusting, two-way communications. It then looks at the five essential, results-driven communication tools that will deliver optimal results. Finally, it gives you some ways to smash through four of the most common communication barriers that can keep you from reaching the success and happiness you desire.
- *The Secret of Negotiating to Make It Happen.* Often the key to securing the help and cooperation you need from others in order to make your Personal Plans happen. The Secret of Negotiating shares the Seven Guidelines GEMs follow to prepare for negotiations and the Ten Negotiating Techniques they apply during negotiations that give them an added edge. The information shared in this Secret will guide you in creating a winning negotiating style all your own.
- *The Secret of Creativity to Make It Happen.* The ability to create and embrace new ideas to enhance your ability to make your Personal Plans happen. GEMs are masters at

using the Secret of Creativity to solve problems and open doors to new ideas. This Secret gives you some ways to overcome the Seven Obstacles of good time management that keep you from giving energy and attention to your creative ideas so that you can make them happen. Then discover the Eight Creativity Boosters that GEMs use to enhance and nourish their creative abilities.

- *The Secret of Changing Course.* What to do when your best-laid Personal Plans fail to meet your objectives. The Secret of Changing Course reveals the approach GEMs take to figure out what went wrong and how to make the needed course changes to get back on track and effectively realize the dreams in their Personal Vision. There are two key elements to successfully changing course. First, you will learn how GEMs review and revise their Personal Vision Statements, SWOT Statements, and Personal Plans and look for needed course changes. Then you will discover how to identify and overcome the roadblocks that can thwart you in making successful course changes.

Without the sense of direction and the power you will gain from the Seven Secrets, you may fall short of finding the true happiness you seek. Collectively, the Seven Secrets will force you to go in the direction that leads to your dreams of what you want in life and in work. The Seven Secrets are practical, they do not take an overwhelming time commitment, and they are not intimidating to use. The more you make use of the Seven Secrets, the greater your chances of creating a life filled with success and happiness.

Now, let's look at your future!

CHAPTER 1

THE SECRET OF
A PERSONAL VISION

Mark is the owner of a successful Web site design company. He is married to a wonderful woman and has two children whom he loves. Not long ago Mark expressed to me that although everything in his life seemed perfect, he felt a very distinct dissatisfaction with the course his life was taking. When I asked what his Personal Vision of happiness and success was—the precise destination he saw for his dreams—Mark just shrugged and said, "I don't really have one. I pretty much just take it day to day."

Most people have some general idea of the future they would like to be living, but few of them take the time to clearly identify the vision of their dream future much less put that vision into writing. In contrast, GEMs are masters at clearly identifying their Personal Vision of happiness and success. At The Alternative Board, we believe that once identified, you should put your Personal Vision down in writing to map out the destination of the happiness and success you desire.

Can you clearly define what you see when you envision your future? Do you know what it would take to be able to say, "What a wonderful life I am living!" Do you know what reflections on your life will bring you greatest satisfaction on your last day on earth? This chapter will help you answer these questions and provide the basis you need to create a Personal Vision Statement that reflects the unique future of your dreams.

A Long-Range Dream

Using the Secret of A Personal Vision as a guide, Mark successfully examined the different arenas of his life and wrote the following Personal Vision Statement:

- Pay off the loan on my home.
- Have a $50,000 annual income from investments that allows me to maintain my current lifestyle.
- Do only those activities at work that I enjoy such as selling to major clients without a lot of out-of-town travel.
- Spend several weeks a year traveling with my wife.
- Spend a lot of time exploring outdoor activities with my children.
- Feel a sense of accomplishment in my music and continue my astronomy studies.
- Sell my business eventually to an outside party and retire with my family to California.

Mark created his Personal Vision of success and happiness based on his long-range dreams. Similarly, your Personal Vision should remain relatively constant for 5 to 10 years into the future. Of course, as you age and the dynamics of your life change as they inevitably will, you may find your dreams for the future also change. No doubt your current dream for the future is much different from what it was 10 years ago, and it is different from what it will be 10 years from now.

The Pinnacle and the Foundation

Imagine a pyramid with the broadest blocks forming the pyramid's base, or foundation, and a single, slender block forming the pinnacle. Initially, most of us jump to the conclusion that our dreams for the future, our Personal Vision, should be viewed as that top pinnacle for which to reach. But without a proper foundation, your dreams may cave in, leaving you emotionally and financially injured. Your Personal Vision therefore must be both the pinnacle and foundation of your dreams.

Another way to understand the importance of your Personal Vision as a foundation is to look at the principles of weight lifting. When I integrated weight lifting into my conditioning program, one of the first things I learned was the importance of having a core foundation. Foot and knee positions are essential; knees must be bent, buttocks tucked under, the lower stomach tightened to support your back, and your shoulders must be back and down. This core foundation allows you to build muscle and, ideally, to lift more weight. The results of strategically living your life, just like lifting weights, will not be properly achieved without a proper foundation.

> **You are creating the solid foundation on which you will eventually build. Do not attempt to develop any plans or implement any major actions for your future prior to completing your Personal Vision Statement. To do so will rapidly lead to failure.**

Pocket Vision

Part of Mark's Personal Vision is to eventually sell his business and retire to California. This aspect of Mark's Personal Vision takes into account the fact that his children may still be living at home when he retires. After Mark and his wife identified this Vision and formulated the plans to make the dream possible, they chose to not inform their preteen children of this eventual move as they felt doing so would unnecessarily upset them.

You may find that your Personal Vision Statement includes some ideas or information that you decide not to share with some or all of your family, friends, and employees. I refer to the parts of your Personal Vision that you choose not to share as your "Pocket Vision®."

One business owner, after hearing a GEM Power Talk I gave to a group of business owners, initially reacted negatively to the concept of a Pocket Vision that's not shared. He claimed that he shared everything with his employees and considered the idea of a Pocket Vision to be unethical.

I recalled that some years earlier the same man had asked for my advice regarding the best way to position his company for sale in four or five years. When I privately asked him if he had shared his plans to sell the business with his management team, his answer was, "No, I can't do that. I'll lose good people if I do that."

Despite the business owner's initial reaction to the Pocket Vision term, he, like most business owners, had actually already applied the concept. He just did not recognize it as such. Even those business owners who say that their Personal Vision is an "open book" and that they share everything with their family and employees usually find out that they have a Pocket Vision when they take an honest look at what they choose to share and what they don't. For example, most business owners do not share their Pocket Vision for selling their business with most, if not all, of their employees. It is also common for business owners to decline sharing with employees their plans to bring family members into the business until such plans are imminent.

> **Identify the pocket factors of your written
> Personal Vision by underlining or marking
> them as separate from the nonpocket factors.**

Realistic Aspirations

Mark included paying off the loan on his home and having a $50,000 annual passive income from investments in his written Personal Vision Statement. These aims are currently out of Mark's reach—a factor that will help to keep him motivated—but they are realistically attainable for him.

It is great to have aspirations that challenge you. However, a Personal Vision that is unrealistic, and that is impossible to attain, creates inevitable failure and will have a negative impact on your efforts. Once completed, review your Personal Vision Statement and eliminate any factors if the chance of achieving them is unrealistic.

A desire for a net worth of $10 million by age 50 may be realistic for a small number of people, but it is not for most. Ask yourself what is realistically attainable if things go really well. If this turns out to be $10 million, wonderful; make it part of your Personal Vision. But if it turns out to be less, don't put in $10 million just because you would like to have it. The challenge is to stretch your dreams so they give you something essential to work toward that is also possible to achieve.

False Assumptions about What Appears to Bring Happiness to Others

In 1860, a gunslinger rode into a tiny Colorado town. On a few of the town's buildings he noticed painted targets with a bullet hole through the center of each one. Impressed with the apparent skills of the shooter, the gunslinger walked into the town bar.

He ordered a drink and asked the barkeeper, "Who is this incredible sharpshooter who hit the center of the targets around town?"

The barkeeper, wearing bottle-thick glasses, squinted and replied, "That was me."

"How is that possible?" the gunslinger asked.

"Easy," said the barkeeper. "I got drunk; I took my guns out, and I started shooting up the town. The sheriff saw me and said he would put me in jail if I didn't draw a red circle around each bullet hole!"

This story illustrates a reality that became all too clear as I was interviewing successful business owners for my nationally syndicated column *Business Insights*. Most people view successful business owners as living happy and wonderful lives. As I discovered, some of them were doing just this. These are the GEMs whose experiences and methodologies I have incorporated in this book. Others, although they appeared to be living happy and fulfilling lives, were anything but happy. Although they were masters of their businesses, they were not masters of their personal lives and did not qualify under my definition of a GEM.

Financial and Material Success

One man I met at a Secrets of GEMs workshop I presented wrote that his dream was to pay off the mortgage on his home, have $1 million in liquid funds to ensure his financial independence, and retire with an annual passive cash flow of $250,000. At the same workshop, another man wrote in his Personal Vision Statement that he wanted to reach a point at which he could retire while maintaining a passive income of $50,000 a year from investments and Social Security—an amount he felt he needed to sustain his lifestyle. The wide range between the desired financial retirement levels of the two attendees points out that material desires differ greatly depending on the individual.

Not surprisingly, when asked about the rewards they desired as a result of their efforts, most people mention materialistic things first. All GEMs list some aspect of a desired financial standard of living in their Personal Vision Statements.

Your Personal Vision may include items you desire but do not need in order to be happy. What items or level of material success do you dream about? How much money or cash flow will bring you the financial freedom you need to live your desired lifestyle? If your want is great and you don't get it, you can still obtain all the happiness you desire from your Personal Vision. But if your need is great and you don't satisfy it, you probably won't be happy. Most of us have no doubt experienced excitement about the prospect of owning an item we see in a store or advertisement even though we do not need it. Want versus need, to a large degree, is a matter of attitude.

Want versus need cannot be measured, but most of us know how to tell the difference. We may want a Rolls-Royce, but we know we will still be able to live a happy life if we don't get one. Your dreams for the future may include things you want to have but you do not necessarily need. Realizing a dream that your company will go public may not be a need for your happiness even though it is something you want.

One way to help identify the material factors you need versus want is to imagine that you have just won the lottery. Without the deterrent of not having enough money to obtain them, what material factors would you still need in your life? The remaining factors are your wants. Remember, there is no right or wrong when determining your needs and wants; there are only your own desires to consider.

When writing your Personal Vision Statement, do be specific in stating the amount of annual income, total benefits, and overall net worth that will give you the financial freedom you desire. If your current situation does not provide for your (and your family's, if applicable) desired financial future, decide if you should either downgrade your dreams for the future or seek greater income.

Nonmaterial Success

One man's long-term dream was to become a high-profile multi-millionaire. Due to his ability and single-mindedness, he successfully created a business that dominated the competition and brought him enormous wealth. Eventually he achieved his dream of being a multimillionaire, and he quickly became immersed in the material trappings he could then afford such as a chauffeur-driven Rolls-Royce. But in the race to sate his desire for material things, he forgot all about the nonmaterial things for which he had once felt passion and that had once brought him fulfillment. His marriage and other relationships suffered, and sadly, he discovered a new passion—drug use. Due to his extreme focus on the material factors his success could provide, achieving his dream failed to provide adequate satisfaction in the other important areas of his life.

I cannot caution you enough to avoid overemphasizing the importance of material desires in finding happiness. Material possessions and rewards, while they are important motivators, are rarely enough to bring true personal happiness. Even if your business generates an income to match your Personal Vision of financial success, you may nevertheless find yourself unhappy and dissatisfied if material success is your total focus.

The challenge for most business owners is to strive for wealth without making too great a sacrifice of the other aspects of their dream life. These sacrifices include relationships with family and friends. It is natural to include material desires in your Personal Vision, but to find true happiness, you must also include the important nonmaterial aspects that contribute to the wonderful life you envision in your dreams.

Work Role

One business owner was offered so many millions of dollars for his business that he could not have spent it in several lifetimes.

When, much to my surprise, he told me that he was turning down the offer, he made the following comment: "If I take the money and sell the business, what am I? I am nothing without being the owner of my business."

Your Personal Vision Statement needs to clearly state the role you would like to play in your job, but this role should not be the sole definition of who you are. Many business owners have no clear psychological separation between how they see themselves in a nonwork identity and their work identity. I have also spoken to many people who are not business owners but who still relate what they do at work as being the crux of who they are. Integrating your identity solely with what you do rather than who you are is not healthy because the potential for losing your job or your business is very high. To protect yourself from becoming emotionally devastated by the loss of a business or job, you should develop other facets to your identity.

At TAB, we ask our members who are business owners to think back to when they started their business and recall how they envisioned their lives would be. Ask yourself if you are doing what you imagined you would be doing when you started your company. Do you have the type of family and other nonwork relationships you wanted to build and maintain? Are you enjoying the outside interests like hobbies and travel that you imagined you would be enjoying?

One business owner, John, found his passion waning as his company grew. When asked what he had passion for, he said he much preferred the technical side of the business over the administrative and management side that had been consuming far too much of his time. As a result of writing his Personal Vision Statement, John rekindled his passion and made the best use of his expertise by becoming the CEO/CTO (chief technical officer). He appointed a qualified person to lead the company and assume what for him was the less desirable role of COO.

The most important considerations regarding the position or job description of a business owner are passion and expertise.

Many people are unhappily doing work for which they have no passion. One common reason for this is that their work is what their family programmed or encouraged them to do. Ray Brun, a TAB facilitator-coach in Oakland, California, told me he became a CPA because it was his mother's dream. He hated being a CPA, so he decided to look for a new career for which he had passion and that he excelled at doing, and that would bring him happiness. Brun has since become a very successful member of the TAB community. He enjoys what he does at work, and he flies in the clouds when he, or the members of one of his TAB Boards, offers advice that leads to another member's success.

Balance between Work and Personal Life

One attorney who was working for a large, successful law firm found himself regularly working 60 to 70 hours a week. He wrote in his Personal Vision Statement that his dream was to limit his billable hours of work to 40 hours a week and to work out of his house while raising his kids. He is currently living his dream although with much less income than he had been making working at a big law firm. This change is great for him, although it is certainly not something that would apply—or appeal—to every attorney.

Your business or work is an important part of your life, but it should be only a part of your life—not your entire life. Too many business owners are so wrapped up with work that they neglect to develop outside interests and fail to see the impact this has on their personal life, including their family and their nonwork relationships. The dreams and goals that prompted them to start their business in the first place, along with other interests, hobbies, and friends, got lost in the work shuffle. Their life became their business, and their business became their life.

When you are working 10 to 15 hours a day—as many business owners do—it is easy to fall into the trap of saying that at some point in the future you will have the time to take care of family and other matters. Too often that time never materializes. On top of this, working long hours on a continuous basis often results in an overload that is responsible for bad judgment decisions.

Darrell Crawford, a TAB facilitator-coach in Grand Rapids, Michigan, had a Personal Vision that included taking every Friday off. He decided to become part of the TAB community, in part, because it helped him fulfill this aspect of his Personal Vision.

TAB facilitator-coach Kevin Armstrong shared the following maxim regarding spending too much time at work: "The more you work 'in' your business, the less it is worth."

Your work and nonwork lives are inherently "in competition" with each other, especially when both are compelling, exciting, and rewarding. It will take discipline on your part to create the needed balance, but you won't get where you want to go until your work and your nonwork lives are synergistic.

GEMs are masters at creating a balance between their personal and work lives. They know the importance of taking time away from business to clear their minds of the day-to-day interference and clutter. As a result of this time away, they do a better job as the catalyst of their life and business.

Tim McGraw has a song, "Live Like You Were Dying." I imagine the words are especially meaningful to him because his father, Tug McGraw, died of brain cancer at the age of 59. One of the hardest balancing acts is finding the right balance between living as if you were dying and living for a dream in the future. You need to determine how much is enough. Define your dreams with the awareness that you can enjoy the fruits of your achievements to their fullest extent only when you have the time and the health to enjoy them.

It seems to me that for many people no dollar figure is ever enough and that there is always a higher goal for which to reach. No one can predict tomorrow and what it will bring. No one knows how long, and of what quality, the remainder of his or her life will be. We do know that we won't be around forever and that the older we get, the more likely it is that physical challenges will arise to keep us from enjoying our dreams.

Think hard about what you really want to do with your time and your life both now and in the future, and include this in your written Personal Vision Statement. You may want to be fully involved with your work, but you may want to work only a few days a week. You need to find a balancing point between taking the time to enjoy today versus investing your time today in your business so you can have more things in the future.

Your Personal Vision Statement should include both the long-term time involvement you desire to spend at work and the time you desire to be away from work. Integrating your personal life and work life is essential because everything you do in your work should build toward achieving happiness in your personal life.

As your business achieves greater and greater success, you may find that the work ethic which was instilled in you during your upbringing prevents you from taking time away from your work. I have also often heard business owners say, "If I take days off, or come in late, my employees will resent my work ethic or reduce their own work ethic."

It often takes a conscious effort to organize your business life so that you can be away from it without worry and to not feel guilty about taking time to enjoy your life outside your business. TAB facilitator-coach Ray Brun says that most of the over 50 members of his TAB Boards have expressed to him at some time feeling guilty that they are "goofing off" while everyone else is working. However, by talking it over with their fellow TAB Board members, they were able to work through the guilt and accept that taking time off is one of the rewards of having taken the risk of owning their own business.

My Personal Vision Statement states that I am available only at certain times during the week for TAB-related communications and other work on TAB matters except for communications with my son-in-law, Jason Zickerman. My Personal Vision Statement also states that I will spend most of my work time via telephone or e-mail so that I am not required to physically be in the TAB office on any set days. At other times, I am available to employees only for emergencies or when I call in to the office. I refer to my time away from The Alternative Board as my "Free-Thought Time." My Personal Vision Statement includes the fact that I do not want to be involved with TAB's day-to-day operations—and I am not.

The Alternative Board has helped me attain my dreams with respect to work involvement. It also integrates, and is synergistic with, the non-work-related elements in my Personal Vision Statement.

Psychic Rewards

One day while waiting for my flight at the airport, a TAB member approached me and asked if I was Allen Fishman. I replied that I was and that I recalled meeting him at a TAB Board meeting I had attended years earlier. He then, rather emotionally, told me that TAB had saved his life. Over the years I had many members of the TAB community tell me that their TAB membership had enriched their quality of life, but never had anyone told me that that it had actually saved his or her life.

This man, however, recounted to me how his life had previously been utterly "down in the pits." Major personal problems were greatly affecting his family life and negatively impacting his business. He had seriously questioned whether living life this way was really worth it.

He said that his fellow TAB Board members, recognizing the depth of his depression, had really reached out to him during this time. They scheduled breakfast and lunch meetings with him, and they continually called to see how he was doing and offer good advice. He said that it was because of their support that he made it through this incredibly difficult time in his life. On a much more joyous note, he went on to tell me that his business was now doing very well and the family problems that had plagued him were now under control.

At the time I created The Alternative Board, one of the factors in my Personal Vision Statement involved the work-related values and psychic rewards I desired. These included the following:

- TAB has to bring benefit to the lives of others. (I get a joy that cannot be quantified when members tell me how TAB has helped make their lives better.)
- The services or products delivered by TAB have to make a positive difference in people's lives and satisfy a real need. (I didn't want to be involved with a service or product just because it would be easy to make money selling it.)
- TAB has to have the potential of becoming internationally significant.

This psychic factor in my Personal Vision Statement has been satisfied beyond my wildest expectations.

The rewards that come from the psyche when you have found peacefulness and contentment or when you feel you have done something worthwhile that has helped others can be of great importance in having a life that is fulfilling. Ask yourself what values and psychic rewards motivate you and bring you a sense of good feeling and peacefulness. Remember, no one other than you can make a judgment about the values and psychic rewards you want from your life. Incorporate the values and psychic rewards that give you the greatest joy from both your work and nonwork lives into your written Personal Vision Statement.

Personal values are those interests, goals, and preferences that guide your personal and business lives such as independence, knowledge, appreciation of beauty, and service to others.

One Realtor included in his written Personal Vision Statement a desire that upon reaching a certain level of success, he wanted to work with only those parties he respected and with whom he enjoyed spending time. Since attaining that level of success, he has declined representing many property sellers and buyers. He has given up opportunities to generate significant revenue because he will not work with certain people. In turn, he has created a work environment that brings him the psychic reward of peace of mind.

It may be important for you to possess political influence or to be honored by the business community for your achievements. Consider the humanitarian and political interests that could bring you psychic reward and whether they factor in to your written Personal Vision Statement.

Are there important spiritual elements in your life that create conflict with your work? Perhaps you would prefer not to work on Sabbaths and religious holidays. Will painting, music, or some other activity bring you psychic pleasure? If so, include these things in your written Personal Vision Statement.

Also think about the areas of personal growth and education that integrate well with your work. What about the fulfillment of your ego, or the quest for more knowledge through some personal achievement such as earning an MBA? I have a neighbor who had a dream to earn an MBA after retiring, and he went for it. These are all important factors to consider when creating your written Personal Vision Statement.

At The Alternative Board, we recommend that Personal Vision Statements include the values and personal qualities that those writing the statements expect themselves to have as well as their family members and their employees. My Personal Vision Statement includes my desire to associate only with people who operate with honesty and truthfulness. What values do you admire and admonish in others? In answering this question, take into consideration your own values and the types of personalities with which you are most comfortable and productive. For example, do you prefer to be around those who are not given to extreme highs and lows? Are you more productive when surrounded by those who challenge your views? Is it important to you to have department heads who have integrity and who don't play politics? All these psychic factors are potentially very important to your future chance of happiness and fulfillment.

Family Relationships

One man included in his written Personal Vision Statement a desire to travel with his wife in a big RV that he intended to buy after he retired. I asked him if he had shared this dream with his wife. He said, "No, but I am sure that's what she wants too." I suggested that he talk to her about his Personal Vision.

When we met the following month, he told me that he had discussed his Personal Vision with his wife. Much to his surprise, he had discovered that she thought his idea was crazy. She had zero interest in spending time driving around the country in an RV. Instead, she envisioned the two of them spending their retirement living in the mountains, far away from people, where she could do crafts and tend her garden.

If you have a spouse or partner and doing things with that person is important to your Personal Vision, find out if he or she shares your views about what you will be doing together on a long-term basis. If you expect that person to be a part of doing the things that you want to be doing, you must get his or her feedback.

My mom, Esther, always says, "Life is not perfect, but you don't need perfect to be happy." You can have a great marriage or business partnership, but to expect those relationships to be perfect and void of disagreements is just not realistic. Over the years I have known only two couples who stated that they had the "perfect marriage." They claimed to do everything together and to never disagree. Both couples are now divorced.

The relationships I have with my family are extremely important to me. This need is clearly stated in my Personal Vision Statement. In contrast, I have been told by many people how unimportant certain family relationships are to them, and how, for example, some people have little interest in spending time with their children or grandchildren.

Remember, no one has the right to judge any factors in your Personal Vision Statement. There is no rule that says you must enjoy spending a lot of time with your grandchildren. The key is to acknowledge what is important to you and to make whatever that is part of your Personal Vision.

If family time is important to you, the time you spend with family members is a key factor to consider when identifying your Personal Vision. Travel can often put a strain on desired family relationships, and many entrepreneurs have identified a desire to reduce the amount of time they spend traveling out of town in their Personal Vision Statements. John Dini, a TAB facilitator-coach in San Antonio, Texas, told me that he was drawn to the idea of becoming a part of the TAB community because his Personal Vision included less traveling out of town so he could spend more time with his family. Since becoming a TAB facilitator-coach, Dini has been able to facilitate TAB Boards and coach members in the San Antonio area without any out-of-town travel. This allows him the time he desires to spend with his family.

As with other factors in your Personal Vision Statement, give thought to whether the family relationship factors you are considering are a need or a want. One man spoke to me about the impact his daughter's drug problem was having on his life. At first he said that he could not be happy in his vision for the future unless his daughter got off drugs. Later he was able to find peace with himself after he acknowledged that the situation was beyond his control and that his daughter's getting off drugs was a want for his happiness and not a need.

One of the most surprising points to me was a factor in one business owner's Personal Vision Statement for her daughter to control her weight problem. The business owner had to come to grips with the fact that her desire for her daughter to get to a healthier weight was a want and not a need before she could be happy.

Another entrepreneur I know had an extremely successful company but an unsuccessful marriage. She told me that regardless of how much professional success she created, she would never be truly happy until her need for a happy marriage was fulfilled. Her Personal Vision Statement included the factor "Have a happy marriage."

What kind of relationship do you want with your relatives? If there is something missing from your relationships, ask yourself if what is missing is a need or a want and whether what you want is realistically within your control.

Relationships with Friends

TAB facilitator-coach Ray Brun told me that some of his long-time TAB members admit that their only real friends are their fellow TAB Board members. Clearly, the reason these friendships stay strong is the common connection of being business owners.

I went through a period when I did a lot of reflection concerning my social friends. I looked at the positives and the negatives each brought to my life, and I made some major decisions regarding with whom I wanted to spend my time. I included in my Personal Vision Statement a desire to have relationships only with those friends who were genuinely nice people and who did not bring along major negative baggage. I now allocate substantial social time to only a few close friends, and I maintain important but more distant relationships with some others.

Not being able to find the time to spend with friends is a problem to which many business owners confess. You may recognize this as one of your problems, but only you know what you want with respect to social friendships for your future. Determining the type of involvement you want with your friends, and with what friends you want to spend your time and including this in your written Personal Vision Statement, will help you gain a clearer perspective that may result in making important decisions about your current friendships.

Mental and Physical Health

One of my mom's favorite sayings is, "If you have your health, you have the world by the ass!" You certainly want to have good mental and physical health, so your written Personal Vision Statement will not be complete until you include the level of mental and physical health you desire.

Identifying your desired level of health in your Personal Vision Statement is essential because it will force you to consider whether your current behavior and health habits support the level of overall health you desire.

Where You Want to Live

Lou hated living in New York City, but he felt he was unable to move because his business was established there. He told me that he had been thinking of moving to Arizona for years, but he felt that it was just a dream.

Only after he put this dream down in writing in his written Personal Vision Statement did Lou actually develop a Personal Plan that helped him attain his dream. Within three years of starting to use the Seven Secrets, Lou moved to Arizona. He has now created a quality of life there that he finds far preferable to what he had in New York.

If you have a dream of relocating, include it in your Personal Vision Statement. The effect of seeing it in writing will start the ball rolling to get you where you want to go.

Traveling

During a trip to Thailand I met a couple in their late seventies who told me they were starting to live out their dream to see the world. They now had the money and time for frequent trips to exotic places. Unfortunately, some of the explorations they had always dreamed of required levels of physical fitness that were too challenging for them due to recent health problems.

Many people's Personal Vision Statements include a desire to travel. You may dream of taking extensive vacations to exotic locations, or you may desire domestic travel that includes time to spend with family and friends. If the type of travel that is a part of your dream future requires a certain level of health, it is important to consider that level of health when you write your Personal Vision Statement.

Retirement

When I was 45 and just realizing my dream of semiretirement to the Aspen, Colorado, area, a friend of mine, who is only a few years older than I am, told me he had just turned down the chance to sell his business for an amount in excess of $5 million. After some consideration, he concluded that he desired a greater value for the company. He decided not to sell and instead to work hard at growing his business for another 15 years before selling it. He planned for a retirement time much later in the future when he could finally sit back and enjoy the fruits of his labor.

When he was in his mid-sixties, he sold the business for many millions of dollars more than the $5 million plus he would have received if he had sold the business when he was in his forties. Unfortunately, he also died of cancer a few years after the sale. After he found out about the cancer, he told me that he wished he had retired at the same time I did. He said that he always thought there would be so many more years ahead to enjoy retirement.

If retirement is something you are thinking about—or should be thinking about—you need to include the timing for your retirement in your written Personal Vision Statement. The right time to start thinking about when you want to retire is a very individual decision that ties in with different factors in your life. I started to plan for my retirement before I was 40. I knew I wanted to be at least semiretired between the ages of 45 and 50. This was due, in part, to the fact that my father died of cancer when he was only 59. His death made me more aware of wanting to take advantage of enjoying my life to the fullest.

Barba Hickman, a TAB facilitator-coach in Boulder, Colorado, shared the following story with me about a CEO who had worked for 40 years in his business. He had a dream to retire at a specific age. He and his wife had retirement plans to play a lot of golf. He also wanted to do some work helping friends or family with their businesses. Unfortunately, he had a severe heart problem that required major surgery just before he retired. The doctors told him that the stress he had been under for many years had largely contributed to his health problems. He realized that his nature made it impossible to be involved in owning a business without having stress.

After retiring, he focused on three things: his marriage of over 40 years, golf and/or exercise, and growing, cooking, and eating healthy food. He has been retired now for over 20 years and is in the best physical condition of his life. He and his wife golf as many days a year as possible, traveling to warmer climates as necessary. But not one day of those 20 years has he worked in business. His experience taught him the importance of having nonwork interests to keep busy within retirement.

It is important when writing your Personal Vision Statement to factor in any desires to embark upon nonwork interests that will take the place of your work interests following retirement. Equally important is not tying your self-worth to your business contributions. When he retired, one friend of mine sold his company that had been grossing over $150 million a year in sales. He retired to the Aspen area with many millions of dollars and quickly became depressed.

His ego had rested largely on the prestige he had earned from being the owner of a business. When he retired, he felt that an important part of his identity was gone because he no longer owned a business. He also missed having something to look forward to for which he felt passion. In addition, all of his social friends were business-related friends, and by selling his business, he had severed these longtime ties. He told me that he felt like an outsider when his friends talked about work because he no longer had anything to talk about. He found happiness only after making some major changes in his life that included developing new interests and finding a new purpose—namely, painting—that replaced his lost passion for his work.

Retirement should be viewed as a new beginning rather than an end. GEMs who elect to retire see retirement as a chance to develop new dreams and travel unexplored roads, just as my friend has developed his passion for painting.

Oswald Viva, a TAB facilitator-coach in Phoenixville, Pennsylvania, has a TAB Board member who included a dream of retiring to California to grow grapes for the wine industry in his written Personal Vision Statement. Consequently, the member developed an exit strategy that included selling his business to his most trusted employees while still retaining an interest in the business. As soon as the member's plan was finalized, he started working on achieving his goals by buying land in the Napa Valley location and meanwhile training the future owners of his business in leading the business.

For many people work is the spirit of purpose that inspires them as their reason to live. What they do at work provides a sense of connection to life on so many different levels that retirement leaves them feeling lost. TAB facilitator-coach Ray Brun says that even his low-handicap golfers admit they can't be happy if all they are doing is playing golf five days a week. Before you decide that you want to retire full time, ask yourself whether doing so will eliminate one of the most important connections you have to your life.

Steve Davies, a TAB facilitator-coach in Long Island, New York, told me about a conversation he had with one of his members regarding exit strategies. The member told him, "I am going to stay in my business—I lack retirement skills." Like him, you may stay in your business, or you may choose to develop a bridge to retirement through part-time work. You may choose to explore a new career option. You don't have to ever plan for a time of no work if you don't want to.

Experts on aging state that those who live beyond 100 embrace, among other things, a reason to live and something that gives them a sense of connection to life. One man, the CEO of a family-owned, western clothing company, went to work every day at 8 A.M. despite the fact that he was over 100 years old. Why would someone still want to work five or six hours a day as the active leader of a business at that age? The answer is that work gives him or her a reason to live and provides an important sense of connection to life, including the personal contact he or she has with the various people associated with that work.

I know many people in the Aspen area who retired after selling very successful businesses—some for many millions of dollars—who became unhappy immediately after retiring. They had a lot of money and free time to do nonbusiness activities, but they felt they no longer had a purpose in life.

One man retired after selling his plumbing supply company for a great deal of money. Five years after he sold his business, he admitted to me that he was tired of not having anything to do that excited him. Prior to retiring, he thought he would spend a lot of time fishing and woodworking. He even built a workshop and spent thousands of dollars on equipment, but he never built anything. Without the meaning and structure of his work life that he had before retirement, he felt zero drive to do anything.

Since then, he has started a new plumbing supply company that operates on a much smaller scale than his former company. He says his happiness has been restored because he is once again doing something he enjoys and at which he is good at doing. His former enthusiasm for living has returned, and because the business operates on a smaller scale, he still has time for fishing and woodworking; activities that he now looks forward to.

Think hard before you opt for a long-term Personal Vision of retirement. Reflect on whether you would prefer to keep your business or remain in your job under circumstances that would allow you to live the lifestyle of your dreams. Many people, including me, have elected an alternative to retirement by retaining less demanding work roles that still meet the purpose and passion of their emotional needs but also afford them the nonwork time they desire.

While writing his Personal Vision Statement, Bill Courtney, who owns HomeSource, a home construction company in the St. Louis, Missouri, area, started questioning whether he wanted to sell his company and retire or keep the business in the family and, in some capacity, still stay involved with the business. He met with his three grown children who were all active in the business, and he asked how they saw their roles in the future. Courtney stated, "As important as the Seven Secrets were to me personally, they were just as important in helping my three children figure out what they wanted."

By working on his Personal Vision Statement, Courtney helped his children to identify that they wanted to keep working in the family business and to pinpoint what each of them wanted to be doing in the business. Courtney decided not to put his company up for sale but to stay involved until his daughter's children were old enough that she could assume a greater role in running the company. He would then pull back on his time involvement but still stay involved in some capacity.

A successful attorney I know had years earlier told me of his plans to retire at age 62. At age 65 he was still not retired. He explained that he still had the desire to spend a few weeks each year traveling to Europe, staying at the best places and eating at the best restaurants. However, he did not have the passive income to do it while still maintaining his standard of living, so he decided to delay his retirement plans.

If you decide that your dream includes a retirement or semi-retirement lifestyle, you need to include how much passive income you will need to support this desired lifestyle in your written Personal Vision Statement. One mistake many people make when projecting the retirement income they will need is that they do not take inflation into consideration. No one can guarantee or predict what the price for anything is going to be years into the future. Based upon past experience, the cost of living will likely be a lot more in the future. Ask yourself what a car cost 20 years ago compared to today to better understand how inflation can impact your retirement cost of living.

Social Security as the sole source of retirement income is not going to be enough in order for business owners or executives to keep the same standard of material living they are used to having. Your Personal Vision Statement should also generally state where the retirement funds will come from, such as from selling the business, IRAs, or a 401(k), to provide for your financial needs during retirement.

Religion and Spirituality

My father's involvement within his synagogue was extremely important to the balance of his life. It brought him great happiness and a good feeling about himself. His dream included being president of his synagogue. For many people in this world, religious or spiritual beliefs bring a great sense of peacefulness and contentment. Only you can decide how important religion is to your dream for the future and how much you want to get involved with it. If your dream future includes a specific type of religious involvement, make sure to include it in your written Personal Vision Statement.

Personal Vision Statements of GEMs

The following excerpts are from the written Personal Vision Statements of several GEMs. These examples will give you an idea of what others have considered to be important for their dreams of their future.

Personal Vision Statement 1

- Reduce my work efforts to no more than 25 hours a week.
- Earn $80,000 in annual income.
- Be a good friend to my three best friends.
- Put aside adequate income that, along with Social Security, will support me in my old age.

- Do a lot of traveling internationally once my daughter goes to college.
- Write and publish a novel.

Personal Vision Statement 2

- Make a minimum of $250,000 in annual income.
- Perform only work activities that I enjoy such as handling media relations.
- Raise my daughter to be a person with good values.
- Spend a minimum of four weeks each calendar quarter on a sailboat with my wife.

Your Personal Vision Statement

Now it's your turn to write your Personal Vision Statement. Use the thoughts and responses you have gathered from this chapter. Remember, your Personal Vision should remain relatively constant for 5 to 10 years into the future, although you may need to alter the vision sooner if a significant change occurs in the dynamics in your life.

Alan Wallach, a TAB facilitator-coach in Milwaukee, Wisconsin, believes that a Personal Vision Statement is most effective when written in the present tense—even if it relates to a future time. Wallach says, "By writing your Personal Vision in the present tense, it will impact upon your subconscious mind because your subconscious mind cannot tell the difference between a mental tape you are playing in the present tense and events that are happening in real time." Wallach further explains, "By activating your subconscious mind, you will become alert to open doors of opportunity that can pull you toward successfully accomplishing your Personal Vision." Wallach likens the process to the pull that takes place when you make a mental decision to purchase a certain make and model of automobile or truck. Once that decision is made, you begin to notice how many of that same make and model vehicle are on the road.

Not having a Personal Vision of what you want out of life is like traveling without clear knowledge of where you are going. It would be like leaving to go to Chicago but instead driving to Springfield. You may enjoy Springfield, but it is not where you really wanted to go.

Some of the items in your Personal Vision Statement will, by their own nature, be date or time specific. For example, you may know at what age you want to retire. It is very common to have a dream of having a certain income by a certain year, or even over a span of several years. Other things, such as being a good friend or raising your child with good values, would be expressed in a more conceptual manner.

Personal Vision Checklist

Before we move to Chapter 2, "The Secret of A Look in the Mirror," let's recap some of the factors that should be considered when creating your written Personal Vision Statement:

- Your Personal Vision is a long-range dream that should remain relatively constant for 5 to 10 years into the future.
- Your Personal Vision must be both the pinnacle and the foundation of your dreams.
- Determine and clearly mark the parts of your Personal Vision that you choose not to share, your Pocket Vision.
- Your Personal Vision must be realistic and achievable.
- What are your needs versus your wants?
- What relationships in your personal and work lives are important to your happiness?

- What balance must exist between your personal and work lives to bring you happiness?
- What values and psychic rewards are important to you?
- What types of work involvement will give you the most pleasure?
- What level of mental and physical health do you desire?
- What are your plans for retirement?
- If you plan to retire, what will you do to fill the time that your work once filled?
- Is travel a necessary element to your happiness?

CHAPTER 2

THE SECRET OF
A LOOK IN
THE MIRROR

Socrates is recorded by Plato in the *Apology* as saying, "The unexamined life is not worth living." While his statement may sound extreme, it certainly holds true that life must be examined and reflected upon if one is seeking happiness and success.

Those who do not make the effort to examine their lives are typically the same ones who don't make the right plans or take the necessary actions to bring greater happiness and success to their lives. In contrast, GEMs are masters at the necessary, in-depth examination required for them to reach their dreams.

During A Look in the Mirror, you will achieve a genuine self-knowledge that will allow you to determine if you personally have what is required to attain each part of your Personal Vision Statement, and whether what you desire for your future is, in fact, a realistic dream. What you uncover in this self-analysis will likely result in the modification, or even the elimination, of some factors in your Personal Vision Statement.

Understanding and Accepting Who You Are

One business owner told me that even after he achieved a level of material success that was beyond his own needs, he continued to work in a way that was, in the opinion of his family members, obsessive. He sometimes struggled with guilt due to the time he spent at work. He rationalized that he continued to work in this manner for the material benefit of his children and grandchildren. But after applying the Secret of A Look in the Mirror, he understood that the reason he continued to spend so much time on business deals was that he enjoyed doing so. He accepted that this was just who he was and that it was okay.

In order to do a true self-examination, you need to understand and accept who you are. You also need to distinguish between your own desires and the expectations of others. If people regard you as a highly successful and driven business owner or executive, it is difficult not to deliver that reality to those who watch and admire your life. It takes courage to see yourself for who you really are. The key is remembering that success comes in many different forms.

SWOT

Your Look in the Mirror will help you determine your strengths, weaknesses, opportunities, and threats. This process is referred to as your "SWOT analysis." The results of your SWOT analysis will help you clearly identify—in writing—exactly who you are and what the "real" world in which you exist is like. TAB facilitator-coach Darrell Crawford refers to the SWOT process as a "WOTS up" analysis for self-examination.

While most business owners I have coached have felt at ease while doing their SWOT analysis, there have been those who have felt resistance to getting to know their true selves. Naturally, people don't want to see bad things about themselves. However, realize that the self-awareness brought on by the SWOT introspection brings with it an opportunity to manage problematic personal characteristics. Forge through any discomfort you may experience in working through your SWOT analysis by reminding yourself that only when you are aware of the traits that have the potential to thwart your success can you implement the necessary actions to neutralize or overcome these traits.

During your Look in the Mirror, don't try to address any of the SWOT factors you identify. Later in the book you will learn how GEMs use the information garnered from their SWOT analysis to develop Personal Plans and to make those plans happen.

Strengths

PAVE Your Way to Success: Your Competitive Edge Strengths

I have a friend, Eduardo, who had only a high school education when he started his restaurant and catering business. He sold the business a number of years later for over $5 million. Despite the lack of any formal management or business education, Eduardo's company was successful because he took advantage of his Competitive Edge Strengths.

Unquestionably, Eduardo has a positive passion for interacting with people and a knack for making them want to do business with his restaurant. I suspect he would have been equally successful as an actor or comedian as he loves being the center of attention. It is amazing how people gravitate to him. Eduardo recognized where his Competitive Edge Strengths were (and they weren't in accounting or operational matters), and he used those strengths to create outstanding success.

Utilizing their Competitive Edge Strengths, as Eduardo did, has been a key element behind the success of every GEM I know who has become a multimillionaire through owning his or her own business.

The strengths GEMs identify in their written Strengths Statements go beyond merely stating something like "I am great with numbers." GEMs PAVE their way to success by accessing strengths for which they have **P**assion and **A**ptitude and a **V**ision of the Big Picture Potential and an **E**mpathetic Personality Match (PAVE). Only when a strength fits all four PAVE criteria can it be considered a Competitive Edge Strength. These strengths are the engine that will propel you to success.

Most business owners spend less than 25 percent of their time on business activities involving their Competitive Edge Strengths. In contrast, GEMS, who more than coincidentally are the owners of the most successful privately owned businesses, typically spend at least 75 percent of their time in business pursuits that make use of their Competitive Edge Strengths.

If you focus 75 percent of the time you spend working on your company in areas that use your Competitive Edge and keep all other activities to 25 percent or less, your company will make great strides forward and you will get more satisfaction from your involvement in the business.

Look First for Passion

My wife and I attended a large party soon after we moved to the Aspen, Colorado, area. Many of the attendees at the party owned very successful businesses. One woman, who knew nearly everyone at the party, commented to me that all the business owners at the party had one thing in common: "Every one of them, regardless of what it is they really enjoy, goes after it passionately."

Without passion, you can have all the ability in the world but still be unable to achieve your dreams. Using the strengths for which they feel passion is a major factor that separates GEMs from less successful business owners. Many years ago my father told me, "People who dread going to work usually fail, so pick a profession, or business, that makes you excited to get up and go to work." His advice zeroed in on the need for passion.

When I was still an undergraduate, I worked in a local accounting firm. The partners told me that I had an outstanding aptitude for accounting, and they offered me an early partnership if I would go with them after graduating. The only problem was that I hated doing accounting work. I was good at it, but I had no passion for it. Consequently, I dreaded going to that job.

Often we excel at doing the things we enjoy. However, there may be areas in which we excel but for which we have no passion. If this is the case, performing these functions can often feel like torture. Such negative feelings are a clear sign that these abilities are not Competitive Edge Strengths.

Going to work each day can be anything but enjoyable if you do not have passion for the kind of work you are doing. You will also find increasing stress in your work responsibilities if your work involves doing things for which you feel no passion. Consequently, you will not give your maximum effort to achieve results. At best, you will be bored and unhappy. At worst, you will fall into a depression and be unsuccessful. Regardless of how great you are at something or how much ability you have, if you don't enjoy doing it, you will not put your heart into it, and the results will not be your best.

When you have passion for what you are doing, you may wake up in the middle of the night with new ideas. You may willingly spend long hours struggling to find the solution to a problem. You are motivated to do these things because you love what you do—not because someone is telling you that you have to do it.

Passion for doing some activities can become all consuming, but I have never met a GEM who suffered from burnout. This is because in addition to doing things for which they feel passion, GEMs appropriately delegate those functions they abhor.

If you have passion for what you do, you have the first intangible that defines a Competitive Edge Strength. Passion is the key element in the formula for success adopted by most happy people, not just GEMs. My daughter, Michele, taught high school for a while before she decided to go to law school. She did well her first semester at law school and was part of the way into her second semester when we had a conversation about her studies.

She told me how stressful she found law school. She felt the core reason for this was because she really did not care about it. We started talking about her passions, and she contrasted her disinterest in law to the great personal satisfaction she had found in teaching. While she found herself procrastinating when it came to her law studies, she had often had to fight herself from spending too much time preparing for teaching.

We discussed the situation in depth over the next few weeks, and she decided to drop out of law school and go back to teaching. As a schoolteacher, her income will never remotely match that of a successful attorney, but Michele loves what she does and has never looked back with regret.

Look Next for Aptitude
One woman who was thinking about joining The Alternative Board owned a service company with her husband. She told me that there was no area in which she was outstanding and questioned if she had anything of value to offer a TAB Board. After speaking to her husband about her, I saw a much brighter picture of her aptitudes. Her husband told me that she had remarkable people skills and that she was a natural leader who easily got her employees to do what she wanted. She did join TAB, and she brought great value as a member due to her insights and advice on creating a great work culture and getting the most out of employees.

It is a very rare individual who is outstanding in all areas of business. When identifying your Competitive Edge Strengths, look for your strongest aptitudes. These should be fairly easy to identify when looking in the mirror. Most of us know the areas in which we excel—and can do better than most. But if you are like the woman mentioned above and cannot see your own abilities whether analytical, verbal, or otherwise as they compare to the abilities of others, ask those around you such as family, friends, or those you work with what they think are your greatest strengths.

Is There a Vision for Big Picture Potential?

One man owned a software company that had grown to $10 million in annual sales. However, those sales had remained flat for three years. During a coaching session aimed at addressing this problem, he told me that before he started his business, he had been a financial officer for another company. While in that position he had enjoyed and been quite successful at mergers and acquisitions. He mentioned that there was currently great opportunity for buying companies in his field but that doing so would take a lot of time, which he did not have.

I asked him to come back the next week with an outline that identified any work activities on which he spent more than 20 hours a month. It turned out he was spending 20 to 30 hours a month helping to prepare his company's financial statements— even though he had a qualified accounting staff. He was spending a lot of hours doing something for his company that he was good at and enjoyed doing but that had no Big Picture potential. When he looked in the mirror, he realized that he should instead be using those 20 to 30 hours a month for his Competitive Edge Strength in mergers and acquisitions. This was an activity that he was good at, enjoyed doing, and that had definite potential to bring Big Picture benefit.

If what you perceive as a Competitive Edge Strength does not have Big Picture potential, it is not a Competitive Edge Strength— even if you have passion and aptitude for doing it. Which of your areas of passion and aptitude have the most potential to help you gain the greatest results from your work activities?

Is There an Empathetic Personality Match?

One woman, Sandy, told me a fascinating story about the struggle she went through in order to realize, and accept, that her personality was part of how she was biologically wired. Sandy had always been extremely outgoing. This behavior had been a continual problem while growing up as it clashed with the expectations of her mother and her mother's family. She could barely remember a time when she was not in trouble with her mother and stepfather, both of whom were very reserved in nature.

When, at age 42, she met her biological father for the first time, Sandy found that she not only looked like her father but that she had also inherited his outgoing personality. Realizing this fact allowed her to embrace her own outgoing personality instead of viewing it as something she needed to hide. She identified her outgoing personality as one of her Competitive Edge Strengths.

Your Competitive Edge Strengths must be a good fit with your basic personality. If there isn't a match between your natural behavior profile and the kind of things you're doing at work, you will counter your natural behavior and create stress in your life. The greater the gap between your natural behavior and the behavior you need to assume to do your job responsibly, the unhappier you will become. Bottom line: you need to do what you are.

What is your basic personality or behavioral nature? It is crucial that you are honest with yourself about the natural you (the personality or behavior you were born with) versus the adapted you (the personality or behavior you assume to survive). Without knowing the natural you, you will be unable to access the plans you need to reduce stress in your life and do work that fits your natural behavior.

One way to help identify the natural you is to use a personality or behavioral survey. These surveys are widely available at a small cost, and they can easily be completed in 10 to 15 minutes. Many of them work off a DISC model that identifies natural behavior as it involves dominance, influence, steadiness, and compliance.

Nonwork Life Strengths

One GEM, Brian, identified the following as his nonwork Competitive Edge Strengths:

- Strong marriage and continual support from wife
- Close relationship with children and grandchildren
- Self-motivation
- Deeply rooted spiritual beliefs
- High energy level
- Good cardiovascular health
- Weight under control

GEMs don't limit the identification of their Competitive Edge Strengths to their business lives. Identifying the strengths outside your work life that meet the PAVE criteria is essential in creating the happiness and success you seek. Examine your personality, good health, outside support systems (including friendships), and any other nonwork elements that could be part of your nonwork Competitive Edge Strengths.

Examples from Competitive Edge Strengths Statements

The following are excerpts from the Competitive Edge Strengths Statements of two GEMs:

Competitive Edge Strengths Statement 1
- Enjoy creatively solving company problems
- Secure recognition for the company by speaking before trade associations that include potential customers

- Maintain and develop strong relationships with key account customers
- Communicate effectively with employees
- Apply sense of humor when under pressure

Competitive Edge Strengths Statement 2
- Creative in developing operational procedures that improve efficiency, thereby reducing expenses
- Create a team atmosphere
- Able to get business financing
- Have ability to excite employees
- Enjoy multitasking

Part of My Competitive Edge Strengths Statement
- Creative and innovative in developing new plans, solutions, and process-oriented systems
- Understand what business owners need to succeed; develop business educational products to serve those needs
- Enjoy strategic planning involvement with TAB
- Facilitate meetings and coach well
- Effective at being a spokesperson for TAB
- Stable marriage and relationships with family and friends
- Healthy

Now identify your Competitive Edge Strengths in writing.

Competitive Edge Strengths Checklist

Before we move on to identifying your weaknesses, let's review the following important factors regarding your written Competitive Edge Strengths Statement. Remember that Competitive Edge Strengths can exist in both your work and nonwork lives.

- Do you feel passion for the strengths you have listed as your Competitive Edge Strengths?
- What are your greatest aptitudes?
- Do the strengths you have listed as Competitive Edge Strengths have Big Picture potential?
- Is there an empathetic personality match between your natural behavior and the strengths you have listed as your Competitive Edge Strengths?

Weaknesses

Creating a Weaknesses Statement that details the elements that limit your chances of success is one of the most important parts of your Look in the Mirror. Conducting an inventory of weaknesses means looking at those things you do the least well, as well as the negative patterns in your life. It is important to make this inventory because you can't neutralize a lack of aptitude or change a negative pattern without first identifying it.

Every GEM has identified his or her weaknesses, and each of them has become an outstanding success in spite of them. That knowledge should serve as an inspiration to those who feel they cannot succeed because of their weaknesses. One way GEMs combat their weaknesses is by not competing in the areas where their weaknesses are important to success. Another method to combat your weaknesses is to take the necessary steps to neutralize them.

Sometimes we are unaware that our weaknesses exist. Ask different sources including your spouse or partner, friends, and/or employees or coworkers what they consider to be your weakest areas and make a list of their comments. Pay special attention to weaknesses that are identified by several sources, even if the weakness appears to be worded in a slightly different form. These are the weaknesses that should warrant your immediate attention.

The following explores several common weaknesses that have been identified by GEMs in their Weaknesses Statements. Take these weaknesses into consideration when creating your own Weaknesses Statement.

Mismatch between Who You Are and Your Work Responsibilities

A business owner, whom I will call Tom, did not like conflict and avoided it. Tom had an assistant who annoyed him to the point that he wanted to terminate her, but he "just couldn't do it." During one coaching session, he told me how her unreliability wasted his time and cost him efficiency. I recommended that he write down all the things about her that annoyed him and then start to resolve the problem by reviewing her and putting her on written notice. I also suggested that he tell her that she either had to change her ways or she would be fired. He committed to that plan of action.

At our next meeting, Tom updated the happenings at his company, but he didn't mention anything about his assistant. When I asked, he sheepishly replied that before he'd had a chance to discuss the issues with her, she had asked him for a raise. I asked if he had used that as an opening to put her on notice.

"No," said Tom. "I gave her the raise."

To think that it is possible to change the essence of who we are is unrealistic. One of the basic laws that permeate each of the Secrets is that we are who we are. It is possible, however, upon recognition of our own weaknesses, to create plans that get results without trying to bring about changes to our basic personalities.

Burnout is a commonly identified weakness that is often a symptom that you are doing things for which you have no passion. When you spend the majority of your time doing what you love, burnout will disappear. In contrast, burnout tends to perpetuate itself. In fact, not only will work burnout create major negative ripples upon your life, but it is also contagious. Mental exhaustion and its resulting negative energy patterns created by burnout can spread to those around you.

Observe how narrow or wide the gap is between your passion, aptitude, and personality and what you do at work. If there is a large gap between "who you are" and "what you do," this is a weakness. Granted, you may be able to do your work quite well by adapting to it; nevertheless, it is a weakness to adapt to the negative aspects of your work versus eliminating the gap between what you are actually doing and what you want to be doing.

TAB facilitator-coach Oswald Viva has a member who owns a service business. The member, who is an excellent outside-people person, listed as a weakness that he does not like—and consequently is not good at—dealing with employees. He had always taken the view that personnel issues were a necessary evil of the business and were something that he simply had to put up with because his business was too small to afford a general manager or even an HR person. This weakness, which he identified in his written Weaknesses Statement, was limiting the growth of his business. Once he saw it written down, however, he was able to take steps to deal with it.

Here's another example of business owners who have had weaknesses relating to the mismatch of who they are and the work responsibilities they have had within their companies. One engineer-owner of a manufacturing company had a job responsibility that positioned him as the company leader. Not all business owners should automatically position themselves as the company leader on a day-to-day basis, which was true in this case. In this instance, there was a mismatch between the work responsibilities for the engineer-owner because he was not a natural leader. His inability persisted in spite of the many leadership training courses he took. He was simply an introvert by nature and did not like to deal with people. After taking A Look in the Mirror, he listed the misery he felt when handling "people matters" in his Weaknesses Statement. Writing it down enabled him to deal with the situation in a positive way.

Another business owner identified a mismatch between his management responsibilities and his basic friendly nature. He listed as a weakness that he had become so friendly with his managers that he found it difficult to enforce accountability. His weaknesses included a pattern of taking employees into his confidence on personal or family matters. It is necessary to set boundaries around the types of relationships you have with those who work for you. For him, the more he was viewed as a friend by his managers and employees, the harder it was for him to effectively manage them. His Look in the Mirror enabled him to develop a successful plan to offset his weaknesses in this area.

Imbalance between Work and Nonwork Lives

One business owner identified one of her weaknesses as, "Not having enough time for strategic thinking because I was continually putting out the day-to-day fires of my business." It was no surprise to learn that her company had not achieved any growth in five years.

Many business owners list as their greatest weakness "taking on too much." This weakness often results in their becoming slaves to their businesses. It is also a major reason why many business owners fail to achieve their full potential for success. This effect is every bit as limiting for those who want to get ahead in management. For many people, the need for the sense of importance is fulfilled by being central to what is taking place even though this centrality limits their available time for doing other things at work and also enjoying things outside the workplace.

One long-term TAB member, who grew his manufacturing business from a home-garage operation to a large plant in an industrial park, discovered much about himself—and his company—during his Look in the Mirror. His self-analysis opened his eyes to the fact that he needed to get more enjoyment from his nonwork life. He was finally able to see that he basically had no life outside his business. This weakness of not balancing work life with nonwork life is one of the most common weaknesses listed by business owners.

A businesswoman, who was a partner with her husband in a service company, was prone to openly ridiculing her husband to others by saying such things as, "He doesn't do anything—all he does is delegate." In contrast, she prided herself on the fact that their company was heavily dependent on her skills and experience. Her husband identified the fact that she seldom delegated as being one of his wife's major weaknesses. He felt that their company was failing to succeed because of his wife's inability to recognize that her views against delegation were a weakness. Ultimately, the company dissolved, and the couple moved to another city to take jobs working for other companies.

GEMs know that delegation is essential to maximizing the results they gain from their time. Business owners who permit their companies to become overly dependent on them are highly unlikely to become GEMs. When an overdependence scenario is in place, it is a weakness. As a result, an imbalance is created, and the growth potential of the company is threatened.

One member of a TAB Board facilitated by Oswald Viva owned a high-tech manufacturing company. The member, who is also an engineer, complained that his business was stagnant because he could not handle all the chores of his job, and he had no time for strategic planning and execution. The truth was that his weakness was that he enjoyed the technical side of the business so much that he spent most of his time involved in these activities while sacrificing most of the strategic, sales, and administrative activities.

Being unable to balance the conflicting demands between nonbusiness organization commitments and other personal life activities, like spending time with family and friends, is another common weakness. Many business owners are guilty of overcommitting to charitable boards, political activities, and other demands from outside their business. They make these commitments without giving up any responsibilities in the business to allow them the time they need for these nonwork activities.

Not Spreading the Credit

A flock of geese was getting ready to fly south for the winter. One goose had a broken wing and couldn't fly, so he found a stick and asked two other geese if they each would put an end of the stick in their beaks as they flew south. He explained that his plan was to hold on to the middle of the stick with his beak.

The geese agreed to help him. The three lined up, put the stick in their beaks, and took off on their flight. Later in the journey, another goose noticed the two geese towing the goose with the broken wing and complimented them on their teamwork.

"What a great idea! Whose idea was it, anyway?" he asked.

The goose with the broken wing immediately piped up, "It was my idea!"

By opening his beak to talk, he let go of the stick and quickly fell to his death.

Many business owners and managers have a tendency to view things in an "I" rather than a "we" perspective. Taking all the credit—or assuming an "I" perspective—is a weakness. The chances of a company's reaching its full potential are much greater if the owner is not intent on taking all the credit. The inability to spread the credit is a weakness that is often difficult to identify until someone else points it out to you.

It is a law of counterproductivity that the best way to turn people off is to adopt an "I" perspective. Many businesses have been held back from their potential, and in some cases even destroyed, because of an owner who took credit for everything.

I learned how counterproductive an "I" mentality can be while I was an employee at the May Department Stores Company. The day before a major committee meeting, I presented the officer to whom I reported with a rather novel approach to solving a problem the company was facing. I had spent a lot of time and energy coming up with what I considered to be the solution to the problem.

The officer read my proposal, and we spent hours discussing it. He said he would give serious thought to it. The next day at the committee meeting, he presented my proposal for solving the problem as his own idea. I was livid, but because of the practical factors involved, I could not object during the meeting.

Afterward, I walked into his office and asked how he could have made the presentation of my idea and taken credit for it. His unacceptable response was, "We are a team, and as the head of the team, it is best if shown as my idea." He left no further room for discussion on the topic. It was simply the way it was.

Prior to that incident, I had gone out of my way to always show him in a favorable light by talking him up within the company. After this occurrence, I never again made any effort to help him beyond doing my job.

Lack of Self-Accountability

One of the weaknesses that many business owners have is failing to be self-accountable. This weakness will prevent any business owner from achieving the same level of success as GEMs. The weakness of lack of self-accountability typically exists because there is no one to whom business owners can be accountable beyond themselves. When they plan to do something and it doesn't happen, it is unlikely their employees will hold them accountable.

This very prevalent weakness was one of the reasons I created The Alternative Board. I recognized that business owners are most likely to accept accountability only from their peers or coaches. The TAB process brings this about through monthly board and coaching meetings.

Lack of Competency in Important Business Skills

One business owner in the construction-products area started his business using his Competitive Edge Strength of creating ideas to improve efficiency in home construction. The amount of time he spent brainstorming was fine when he was a very small operator, but it became a problem as his company began to grow.

In doing his Look in the Mirror, he acknowledged that while he was really good at solving construction problems, he was weak at financing, leadership, marketing, sales, and almost all the areas needed to make his company grow. Identifying these weaknesses, and later coming up with Personal Plans for compensating for these weaknesses, was a major factor in growing his company to great success before selling it.

Most of us have competency levels in certain skill areas that are less than adequate. Business owners and managers are often very strong in one or more specific areas, but they do not have expertise in all the areas needed for a company to grow. GEMs recognize this as a weakness and hire people who have these needed skills as soon as their company is in a position to do so.

Poor Health

One GEM who owns a business in the services industry suffered two heart attacks within a few months of each other. The weaknesses he saw in his mirror changed dramatically after this experience. Consequently, following his Look in the Mirror, his company not only succeeded in spite of his health weakness but actually prospered due to a decision he made to bring his son in as president and COO to help counter the stress that was partially responsible for his heart attacks.

There is no way to overstate the importance of recognizing the weaknesses of poor health and poor health habits. No matter how well everything else is going in life, poor health can negatively impact your success. GEMs have identified in their Weaknesses Statements such things as being overweight and having heart problems.

Example from a Weaknesses Statement

The following is an excerpt from a Weaknesses Statement written by a GEM. After the GEM identified her weaknesses and wrote her Weaknesses Statement, she was able to create and achieve plans that brought her increased happiness and great success with her retail chain.

- Spend too many hours each week at work talking with store managers on the telephone
- Not enough of my time is focused on Big Picture activities
- Stress, high blood pressure, and overweight
- Involved in too many political and/or social activities, which leaves too little time for my family
- Constantly defer or avoid healthy activities that I enjoy (like walking) in favor of spending more time working

Everyone has weaknesses. Identify the weaknesses that have the biggest impact on your life, and write them in your Weaknesses Statement. Later in the book you will learn how to develop Personal Plans that take these weaknesses into consideration.

Weaknesses Checklist

Before we move on to identifying your opportunities, let's review the following important factors regarding your written Weaknesses Statement. Remember that weaknesses can exist in both your work and nonwork lives.

- Is there a gap or mismatch between who you are and what you do?
- Is your company overly dependent on you?
- Do too many nonwork commitments demand too much of your time?
- Do you do a poor job of balancing your work and nonwork lives?
- Is yours an "I" or a "we" perspective?
- Do you lack self-accountability?
- Do you lack important business skills that are needed by your business?
- Do you have poor health or poor health habits that could negatively impact upon your success?

Opportunities

GEMs look for opportunities that will make them more effective in strategically living their lives and leading their businesses. Opportunities abound for making significant advances in the quality of life both at work and outside of work. In order to take advantage of these opportunities, it is often necessary to explore beyond the self-imposed boundaries we typically create for ourselves.

GEMs first take the time needed to identify the full scope of opportunities that are available to them. Only after this do they begin to analyze their choices and choose the opportunities they wish to seize. The following are seven common opportunities that have been identified in Opportunities Statements written by GEMs.

Take these opportunities into consideration when creating your own Opportunities Statement.

Common Opportunity 1: Using More of Your Time for Your Competitive Edge Strengths

Remember the software company owner who was spending a lot of time each month doing accounting work on his company's financial statements? When I asked him if he thought this was making the best use of his time, he pointed out that preparing the company financial statements was something that he was really good at and enjoyed doing. He believed that by personally doing the company's financial statements he had a better handle on the company. I pointed out that he had an opportunity to make better use of his time by doing something he was good at, enjoyed doing, and that could also bring Big Picture benefit to his company.

He did not become a GEM until he Looked in the Mirror and saw an opportunity to devote a significant portion of his time to his Competitive Edge Strength of bringing about mergers and acquisitions. This opportunity held the potential to make dramatic improvements in the size and profits of his company that could not result from performing accounting functions that could easily be done by someone else. Using more time for Competitive Edge Strengths that have Big Picture potential is an opportunity identified by many GEMs.

Common Opportunity 2: Turning a Weakness into an Opportunity

A business owner I know expressed to me that he was not as happy as he wanted to be in spite of the fact that his company was extremely successful. He loved his business, but he had a feeling of inferiority whenever he was surrounded by college graduates because he had never finished college. He originally identified his lack of a college degree as a weakness, which helped him to realize that there was also an opportunity to get a college degree while still running his business.

Part of being a GEM is having a life that sparkles and brings about fulfillment on many levels. This man's story illustrates that people cannot be GEMs if their businesses are a success but they are not happy in life, but if they look for opportunities, they can become GEMs. Attending college and eventually getting a degree gave this business owner the fulfillment he sought.

Are there any weaknesses that you have identified that could be turned into opportunities for making major strides forward in your life?

Common Opportunity 3: Taking a Breather and Recharging

After leaving Tipton, I took a three-year break from running a company. I came back refreshed and with more energy than ever to tackle future challenges. The time away from business allowed me to conceive of new ideas for creating The Alternative Board and successfully moving it into what it has become.

Breaks do not have to last years to yield great benefits. One GEM told me that taking one year with a minimum-business-growth expectation was sufficient to refuel him emotionally and resulted in long-range benefits to his company. Taking advantage of his opportunity to slow down for a while allowed him to germinate better ideas for growing the company.

One of the hardest things for driven people to do is to take some time to step back from focusing on moving their company or career forward in order to recharge their inner battery. In contrast, GEMs recognize that the best course of action sometimes is to take a break, even when new business expansion opportunities arise. Just because an opportunity to expand your business exists, it does not mean you should absolutely go after it.

Common Opportunity 4: Spending More Quality Time with Your Family

One business owner saw an opportunity to become very involved with her granddaughter when her grown daughter and young granddaughter moved in with her. She acknowledged that acting on this opportunity would greatly alter her usual way of living and would compromise her time involvement with her business.

Nevertheless, she made a conscious decision to take advantage of a personal opportunity that greatly enriched both her and her granddaughter's lives. She declined taking long trips, either on vacation or business, so she would not be away from her grandchild for an extended period of time. She also chose to turn down new business in order to make time for things like taking her granddaughter to the park and reading to her.

Did she sacrifice business growth and the chance to obtain greater wealth? The answer is yes, but this woman is still a GEM. She is living the life she wants. Her company generates enough money for her to live the lifestyle that she desires while allowing her substantial time with her grandchild.

For those who work for others, taking advantage of this sort of opportunity may require difficult decisions. One woman I know gave up a challenging and high-paid executive position to do freelance work from home until all her children were attending grade school full time. While this provided an opportunity to spend more quality time focusing on her children, it also involved a sacrifice of income and a major setback to her existing career. But the change in her life circumstances also opened up exciting opportunities for new ventures that she might have missed had she remained in her previous career position.

Common Opportunity 5: Becoming Involved in the Community's Civic and/or Political Life

During certain periods of time, I have been quite active in civic and political causes about which I felt strongly. These causes have ranged from being involved in getting voters to approve the funding for a national arch museum in St. Louis to forming a political lobbying organization that, among other things, brought about a state constitutional amendment.

I find that helping to bring about something for which I feel passion brings with it an incredible emotional euphoria. If there are areas that are civically or politically important to you, ask yourself if the opportunity of getting involved on some level will provide you with an emotional reward that is worthwhile in relation to the amount of time and effort you will have to devote to such a project.

Common Opportunity 6: Engaging in Hobbies and Other Fun Activities

In my early forties, and for many years thereafter, it was very important to me to spend a lot of time downhill skiing. Recently I decided to get horses for my family. I have since found myself becoming less interested in skiing and more and more fascinated with learning as much as I can about the "horse world."

It is important to consider hobbies and other fun activities as having the potential for making a positive impact on your life. What hobbies and fun activities appeal most to you?

Some of the hobbies and activities that GEMs have listed in their Opportunities Statements include these:

- Devote more time to painting and getting a show in a gallery
- Write a book and get it published
- Develop photography skills

- Garden (Some feel that relationships will make you happy for a while; but a garden will make you happy for a lifetime.)
- Travel to areas always dreamed of

Identify the hobbies and other fun activities that may have the biggest impact on your life, and include them in your written Opportunities Statement.

Common Opportunity 7: Pursuing Religion and Spirituality

One GEM identified in his Opportunities Statement that he wanted to undertake a theological program of study that would give him a greater understanding of his religion. Another GEM wrote that he wanted to take time away from his successful business to raise money for his church. Although he did not give up his business entirely, the involvement he had with his church really became the center purpose in his life.

As I mentioned earlier, for many people spirituality and religion are important parts of their long-term vision for happiness. There are also short-term opportunities that stem from a desire relating to religion and spirituality that may lead toward a long-range vision in those areas.

Example from an Opportunities Statement

The following example is from an Opportunities Statement written by a GEM who owns a very successful retail chain:

- Take college marketing courses because I have an interest (but not a strong background) in marketing
- Bring daughter into the business
- Improve relationship with spouse, family, and friends
- Improve physical and mental health
- Devote more time to hobbies and other fun things

Now it is your turn to write your Opportunities Statement. Use the opportunities you have identified that, if successfully pursued, will best enhance your work and nonwork lives.

Opportunities Checklist

Before we move on to identifying your threats, let's review the following important factors regarding your written Opportunities Statement. Remember that opportunities can exist in both your work and nonwork lives.

- Is there an opportunity for you to more effectively use your time focusing on your Competitive Edge Strengths?
- Do you have any weaknesses that could be turned into opportunities?
- Is there an opportunity to take a breather and recharge?
- Is there an opportunity to spend more quality time with family?
- Is there an opportunity to become active in civic or political causes?
- Is there an opportunity to partake in hobbies or other fun activities?
- Are there religious or spiritual opportunities that are important to you?

Threats

I have a friend who lives in North Carolina. The hurricanes that hit her area often bring with them the major destruction of lives, homes, and businesses. While she cannot predict when a hurricane or storm will hit, history reveals that every four or five years there is likely to be a hurricane that will hit her area.

She knows she cannot stop the storms, but she can prepare—to some degree—for the threat of a storm. She prepares by boarding up her home and business and removing potential hazards the storms could bring about whenever there are storm warnings. She also has a backup generator ready to go.

You have no real control over a threat, but once something is identified as a potential threat, you can develop ways to react to it should it occur. Creating a Threats Statement helps GEMs identify the threats that have a real chance of occurring and that they cannot prevent from happening, but for which they need to be prepared.

The Chinese symbol for the word *crisis* is made from combining the characters that mean "danger" and "opportunity":

The Chinese Symbol for Crisis

Danger   Opportunity

As the symbol indicates, danger is implicit in crisis, but there is also the opportunity for constructive action. Threats are based on circumstances over which we have no control, so there is no real way to stop them from happening. However, recognizing the patterns and signs that point toward potential threats allows us to prepare a way to handle and react to a threat if it should occur, and possibly even turn a threat into an opportunity.

It all starts with identifying the threats. Things that occur on a trend basis are more likely to happen. Let's look at some of the common threats that have been identified by GEMs. Take these threats into consideration when writing your own written Threats Statement.

Poor Health

I have a friend who has had multiple sclerosis for decades. He takes medicinal shots that fortunately have greatly reduced the frequency and intensity of his MS episodes. Although the cumulative destructive forces of MS episodes are beyond his control, he has identified as a threat the potential for the reoccurrence of an episode. Faced with the very real threat of additional episodes, he has made plans so that he can respond effectively and the episode will not destroy his business.

One health-related threat faced by most business owners is the question of what will happen to the company if they die or become incapacitated. Every business owner needs to look at this threat in his or her mirror and come up with a written disaster plan of how the business will be run or sold if he or she suddenly and unexpectedly dies.

As you grow older, you face increasing risk of health problems. Identify the health risks that are most likely to affect you. Look at any health situations within the history of your family that have potential to compromise your personal health.

Personal Guarantees for Company Loans

One business owner decided not to take on the financial risk of an additional company loan because the bank wanted him to personally guarantee the loan. Declining the loan meant passing on a great business opportunity.

A common threat for business owners is financial risk to personal assets from personal assets pledged or personal guarantees given to a bank for lending money to their companies. GEMs identify the threat to their financial situation from personal guarantees and then determine how much personal exposure they are willing to accept. The amount of risk a business owner wants to take on is often dependent upon the stage and health of his or her company. How you address the threat when identified is your decision, but you can't ignore the need to look at this factor.

Personal guarantees are not limited to business loans and merchandise lines of credit. They also extend to personal credit cards and home loans. If you want a larger home, ask if you are comfortable with the risk of not being able to make your larger mortgage payments.

Before you risk your assets, evaluate the potential gain versus the risk involved and what impact the added stress will have on your life. GEMs generally want to take reasonable risks, but they avoid making a habit of taking a risk simply because an opportunity exists.

Family Difficulties

One business owner told me that his marriage was going badly and although he did not want a divorce, the possibility existed that his wife would file for divorce. The potential ramifications of a divorce called for him to make preparations in case she filed.

After he was served with divorce papers, he followed through with these preparations. He dissolved the law firm he had built and took an easier approach to life by becoming a sole practitioner. The divorce was heartbreaking for him, but having identified the threat before it happened, and having a plan for it if it did happen, allowed him to more easily move forward with his life.

As your children enter their adolescent years, it is common for there to be clashes that create potential threats to your happiness. Anyone who has children should not be surprised that problems often exist in the relationship between parents and their children. You may not be able to stop relationship clashes, but you can mentally prepare yourself for certain types of adolescent action to take place. This will help you get though this stage in your children's lives.

The potential threats that shadow the well-being of those you love carry heavy impact. One business owner had a son and a daughter in the business. The son had a drug problem that had caused major problems not only among family members but also with employees. Although the son was currently off drugs and was being treated, there remained the threat of the problem returning. The business owner wanted the son out of the company if the problem reoccurred, but his wife insisted that the son should remain in the business even if the drug problem came back.

The business owner identified the threat from a relapse of the drug problem in his written Threats Statement noting that a relapse could create a real challenge to his leadership of the company and his family relationships. The situation posed a threat to the man's relationships with his wife, daughter, and all nonfamily employees in the business.

No matter how much love we feel for a parent, the inevitability is that caring for our parents in their old age can create many changes in the life we are accustomed to living. One business owner had a mother who had survived a series of strokes. Even though she was doing well, it was foreseeable that there would soon come a time when she would be incapable of taking care of herself. The identification of this threat resulted not only in a plan for dealing with the obvious financial considerations but also in a plan for dealing with the threat that it would take a great deal of time away from work activities to tend to his mother's well-being if another stroke should occur.

Example from a Threats Statement

The following are excerpts from the Threats Statement of one GEM:

- My parents are aging and could at any time have setbacks that require expensive medical care.

- Personal assets are at risk because of personal guarantees on millions of dollars of company loans.
- My spouse might refuse to sign a personal guarantee needed for a loan to finance the expansion of the business.
- My son who is working in my business is not happy with the working relationship he has with me.
- My daughter's drug problem could recur at any time and drain my emotional energy.

Identify the threats that may have the biggest impact on your ability to live your life to the fullest, and use them in writing your Threats Statement. Remember that you have no real control over threats, but you can control how you prepare for or respond to them if they materialize. Although it is easier said than done, there is nothing to be gained by getting upset or obsessing over things that you cannot change. GEMs recognize that it is a waste of energy worrying about threats. They just do what they can to be ready if a threat should take place.

Threats Checklist

Before we move on to Chapter 3, "The Secret of The Personal Plan," let's review the following important factors regarding your written Threats Statement. Remember, threats can exist in both your work and nonwork lives.

- Do you have any potential health problems that could impact your happiness and success?
- Are your assets potentially at risk due to factors such as personal guarantees of company loans?
- Are there potential problems within your marriage that could impact your happiness and success?
- Are there potential problems with your children that could impact your happiness and success?

- Are there potential care issues with your parents or in-laws that could impact your happiness and success?

What Next?

Now that you have done a self-assessment of the factors that can affect how you get to the destination of your dreams, it is time to review your observations relating to achieving your Personal Vision. You may realize that in light of your Look in the Mirror, unless you gain new strengths, neutralize weaknesses, act on opportunities, or address certain threats with Personal Plans, some aspects of your Personal Vision are not reasonably attainable. At this point, you may wish to go back and modify, or even eliminate, some of the factors in your Personal Vision Statement.

The owner of one jewelry company found the process of A Look in the Mirror so valuable that he urged his family members to create their own written Personal Vision for the future they wanted and to look in their own respective mirrors. His daughter, Linda, took his advice. Her Look in the Mirror brought about an unexpected result.

Linda had won awards for her selling ability and was consistently the top sales achiever in the company. Her Personal Vision Statement indicated that she liked living the lifestyle tied to the high income she was earning at the family business, but her Look in the Mirror clearly identified that she had no passion for sales. She admitted that she found the job extremely stressful and was doing it just for the money.

Linda had a degree in education but had left teaching years prior due to the income limitations. After her Look in the Mirror, she realized how much she missed teaching. Linda revised her Personal Vision Statement to reflect a lifestyle based on the earning ability of a teacher. Despite the monetary life changes such a career change would require, Linda left sales for teaching, a career that was consistent with her Competitive Edge Strengths.

After you have modified your Personal Vision Statement so that it truly reflects what is realistically possible based on your Look in the Mirror, it is time to create the Personal Plans that will bring your Personal Vision to life.

CHAPTER 3

THE SECRET OF
A PERSONAL PLAN

You have now identified your Personal Vision of happiness and success, the strengths and opportunities you have to help you reach that vision, and the weaknesses and threats that may become obstacles to your achieving your dreams. This information is crucial to developing the road map, or Personal Plan, that will lead the way to your dreams.

I live in the Colorado Rockies and am an experienced hiker. The surest way I know to get lost is to hike into unfamiliar terrain without first looking at a map. Running your life without a map or guide is no different. You need a map to reach your dreams or you stand a good chance of getting lost and failing to achieve what you want.

Far too many people are operating without a map. Some may have a general idea of what they want floating around in their mind, or even bits and pieces of a plan written down somewhere, but the plans for how to achieve their vision for their dream future is not mapped out, step by step, on paper.

A common mistake made by most business owners is to rush directly into creating Personal Plans without first taking the time to develop a Personal Vision or doing the SWOT self-analysis. If you've ever watched a construction crew work on a skyscraper, you know that before the concrete can be poured, the steel reinforcing rods must be set and the forms must be in place. After the pouring, the finishing must be done before the concrete sets. This process provides a good physical image of the importance of creating your written Personal Vision Statement and completing your SWOT analysis and written SWOT Statements before creating your Personal Plans.

In this chapter you will learn how to transfer your thoughts and ideas into a series of written Personal Plans that form the style and indicate the direction that will lead all aspects of your life to the success and fulfillment of your dreams.

The Science and Art of A Personal Plan

The Secret of A Personal Plan leads you away from the frantic, idea-of-the-week method and helps to prevent the failures that come from making spur-of-the-moment decisions. GEMs know that planning takes patience. Patience is something that is often difficult for business owners to achieve. TAB facilitator-coach Alan Wallach has found that many of his TAB members execute when they should be planning because they feel that unless they are actually "doing something," they are not getting anywhere.

The planning process takes time. The key to developing any Personal Plan is using a careful approach and giving it your full attention so that it can bring you closer to reaching your Personal Vision. You need to consciously fight against executing when you should be planning. It may take weeks, and it will certainly take at least days, to gather all the elements—in writing—for each of your Personal Plans. It is not how fast you go in creating your Personal Plan that is important—but that you do it effectively.

Because most business owners do not have an instinct for personal planning, they need a structured process to make their Personal Plans. The personal planning process we coach at The Alternative Board evolved from the method I use for business planning. Using this method, which has brought me business successes over the years, seemed to be a natural way to bring about the same level of success in personal planning.

Each of your Personal Plans will contain four elements that must be put into writing in the form of a Personal Plan Statement.

Overview of the Four Elements

Each of your written Personal Plan Statements will contain the following four elements: Critical Success Factors (CSFs), Goals (short-term goals as realistically attainable within 36 months), Strategies, and Action Plans. Your written Personal Plan Statements should be short, concise, and easy to follow, thus creating a clear path of where you want to go and what needs to be done to get there.

> **Focus on developing one written Personal Plan at a time and on getting that Personal Plan well underway to successful implementation before adding any additional Personal Plans. You will learn how to make your Personal Plans happen later in the book.**

Critical Success Factors (CSFs) Statement

Remember the business owner in the construction industry who, after doing his SWOT analysis, identified his weaknesses in certain skills including marketing and sales? He developed a Personal Plan with a Critical Success Factor of hiring someone to be in charge of marketing and sales.

The first element in each of your Personal Plans is a written Critical Success Factors (CSFs) Statement. CSFs are conceptual factors that are so critical to the success of your Personal Vision Statement that you will not find the happiness and success you seek without them. Each of your Personal Plan Statements will focus on solving or satisfying one Critical Success Factor.

A review of your SWOT Statements will help you identify your CSFs. You will find that the most meaningful factors will literally pop out at you as you review these statements. For many people, the first CSFs identified involve a weakness noted in the written Weaknesses Statement. Let's take a look at how some others identified their CSFs.

Tom, whom I mentioned earlier, had a weakness in handling conflicts. This weakness resulted in his giving a raise to an assistant he really wanted to fire. In many ways Tom is a great leader and has great people skills. However, Tom could not change the reality that it was in his nature to avoid conflict. Tom's company could not reach its potential until something was done about his weakness. His fellow TAB Board members convinced him that eliminating this weakness was critical to the success of his company and encouraged him to hire a president to handle all the internal affairs of the company. Tom created a Personal Plan based on the CSF of engaging a president/COO.

Tom's company did not go into its expansion mode until he delegated the responsibility to address conflicts that, if left to him, would not get resolved satisfactorily. As a result of turning over the COO responsibilities to the president, he is now able to exercise his talents by focusing on relationships with outside people, without the weight of dealing with the internal "headaches." His business is in a fast-growth curve, and he is a happy person.

Also mentioned earlier was the business owner of the high-tech company whose weakness was spending too much time on technical matters and not enough time on strategic matters. His TAB Board saw this weakness as a factor that was critical to the success of his company. At the suggestion of his fellow TAB Board members, he hired a qualified engineering manager and a manufacturing manager to whom he could delegate many of the technical responsibilities. Furthermore, with the help of his TAB coach, he is engaged in strategic planning and execution. His business is now enjoying a period of high growth, and he still enjoys his time "playing" in the technical field.

One CSF Focus per Personal Plan

One business owner, Ted, reviewed his SWOT Statements to help identify the factors that were crucial to attaining his Personal Vision Statement. His leadership skills are his greatest Competitive Edge Strength, and he could use these skills to take his company to far greater levels of success. Getting too friendly with his employees was the weakness that was most likely to thwart him in attaining his Personal Vision. His Opportunities Statement clearly indicated that learning business financing techniques was crucial to the attainment of his Personal Vision. Finally, Ted identified being overweight and having high blood pressure from his Threats Statement as a crucial factor that could prevent him from attaining his Personal Vision.

Ted listed each of these SWOT factors as a CSF and then decided that the one he had to focus on in his first Personal Plan was learning enough about business financing to enable him to understand the financing alternatives available to him for growing his company. This CSF was the factor most critical to his future success and happiness. At The Alternative Board, we call this CSF the *Driving Critical Success Factor* (DCSF). Your DCSF is that factor you see as most critical to fulfilling your Personal Vision Statement.

TAB facilitator-coach Oswald Viva has a board member whose written Personal Vision Statement included spending a lot of quality time with his son. The man identified several possible

CSFs that were essential to his Personal Vision Statement, but he determined that spending quality time with his son was his DCSF; the factor most critical to achieving his Personal Vision. This resulted in a written Personal Plan where the CSF was, "Restructure my time needed at the business so that I can spend much more time with my son."

CSFs Statement Example

Your CSFs Statement will list several CSFs. You will choose just one of these, your DCSF, for your first Personal Plan. The Critical Success Factors Statement of one business owner included the following:

- Work fewer hours without giving up success
- Increase use of Competitive Edge Strengths at work
- Create non-work-generated net worth and passive income
- Remove stress from lifestyle
- Help other family members
- Improve personal relationships

CSFs Statement Checklist

After completing your written CSFs Statement and choosing the one CSF (your DCSF) most important to satisfying your Personal Vision, review the following checklist:

- Is your CSF conceptual?
- Is your CSF so critical to the success of your Personal Vision Statement that you will not find the happiness and success you seek without it?

Goal Statement

One GEM had a Personal Plan with a CSF to retire. He wrote the following Goal Statement to satisfy his desire of retirement, "Have my son trained and ready to take over the business within three years so that I can fully retire."

The second element of each of your Personal Plans is the Goal of the Personal Plan. This Goal, once achieved, will satisfy the CSF for your Personal Plan. To help establish the Goal for each of your Personal Plans, first write down several potential Goals. Each of your potential Goals must be specific, be measurable, have a timeline, and be reasonably attainable within 36 months.

It will work to your advantage if your Goals can be achieved within a time frame shorter than 36 months. Owners of small businesses tend to work by deadlines. If you are like these business owners, if you set a Goal to be completed in 36 months that could actually be completed in 12, you may be creating a situation in which you will lose focus. This can easily be avoided by creating realistic Goals deadlines.

When I first created the process for developing Personal Plans, there were short-term, midterm, and long-term Goals. We no longer put Goals in that framework because not only did it prove confusing, but this approach was also overwhelming to those using the process. This complex, multi-time-period approach ran counter to the fact that most of us are able to focus only on Goals that can be achieved within a one- to three-year time span.

Finally, take one last look at your potential Goals, and consider the risks involved in going for them. GEMs may or may not ever gamble in Las Vegas, but when it comes to business, the risks they take in going after a Goal are based on having a certain level of control over the outcome as well as the downside impact if the plan for achieving the Goal does not work.

Choose the one Goal from your list of potential Goals that will have the greatest effect on satisfying your CSF, and use this Goal to create your written Goal Statement for your Personal Plan.

Goal Statement Example

The following is a Personal Goal Statement written by a business owner. Note that this Goal is private and would most likely be kept as a Pocket Goal because most business owners would not share this information with their employees.

- Sell company within 36 months for a minimum price of $5 million, including the building owned by the company.

Goal Statement Checklist

After completing your written Goal Statement, ask yourself the following questions about the Goal you have elected to use in your Personal Plan:

- Is your Goal specific enough so that there is no chance of anyone's misinterpreting its meaning?
- Is your Goal clearly measurable?
- What is the timeline for attaining the Goal?
- Is your Goal realistically attainable within the time period identified above?
- Is your Goal achievable within a 36-month time period?
- Is the benefit to be gained from attaining the Goal worth the risk or downside if you fail to achieve the Goal?

Strategies Statement

A certain level of desired health included in the Personal Vision Statement of one business owner resulted in a Personal Plan that had the following potential Strategies: eating a healthier diet, consuming less alcohol, quitting smoking, starting a regular exercise program, worrying less, handling stress better, managing obsessive behaviors, avoiding taking on other people's problems that tax mental energy, and wasting time mulling over things that happened in the past that she was powerless to change. From this list of potential Strategies, the business owner selected five Strategies to include in her Personal Plan.

The third element in each of your Personal Plans is a written Strategies Statement for achieving the Goal of your Personal Plan. Strategies are conceptual versus measurable and so cannot be—and should not be—quantified. Although it is possible to have only one Strategy for attaining your Goal, it is much more likely that you will need as many as, but not more than, five Strategies for each Goal.

It is easy to come up with many different Strategies for achieving a Goal, but the more Strategies you have, the thinner you will spread your energies and the less focused you will be. One of your challenges will be to limit yourself to a manageable number of Strategies. I have never seen anyone focus on more than five Strategies for a Goal at one time who successfully achieved that Goal.

The following questions will help you develop the Strategies needed to achieve your Goal:

Q: What Strengths need to be used to achieve your Goal?

A: One GEM, Jill, had a CSF to move her company to a much greater level of profitability and a Goal of reaching $700,000 in profits within three years. She responded to my question of "What Strengths do you need to achieve your Goal?" by stating, "To use my strong training abilities to develop additional salespeople needed to expand company sales."

Q: What Weaknesses need to be neutralized to achieve your Goal?

A: Jill responded, "To reduce company dependence on my personally selling company products."

Q: What Opportunities may be capitalized on to achieve your Goal?

A: Jill responded, "Selling additional services to our current clients."

Q: What Threats need to be prepared for in order to achieve your Goal?

A: Jill responded, "Key accounts may not like the new salespeople taking over my selling relationships and as a result may stop giving their purchases to the company."

Q: What out-of-the-box Strategies do you have for achieving your Goal?

A: Jill responded, "To engage independent representatives to sell the company's products to out-of-town clients."

Strategies Statement Example

The following is one of the Strategies from a Personal Strategies Statement developed by a business owner:

• Offer brother who currently works in my business the exclusive opportunity (for a reasonable period of time) to buy the business. If he cannot raise the funds by a specific deadline or if prior to this deadline he gives up trying to raise the funds, list the business with a business broker.

Now it's your turn to write your Strategies Statement.

Strategies Statement Checklist

After writing your Strategies Statement, answer the following questions to check and refine your Strategies Statement:

• Is each of your Strategies conceptual but still clear enough that there is no question of anyone's misinterpreting its meaning?

- Does each of your Strategies avoid measurements and timelines?
- Will each of your Strategies—if achieved—be of major importance to attaining your Goal?

Action Plan Statement

Remember Oswald Viva's member who identified spending more quality time with his son as the CSF for one of his Personal Plans? The Goal of his Personal Plan was simple. He wanted to eat dinner at home four nights a week with his family and to actively be doing so within a 12-month period. His Strategies included delegating his sales training and sales management functions to others. His measurable Action Plan for this Strategy included the following:

- I will promote or hire someone who has outstanding sales management and training ability to become sales manager within six months of today.
- I will interview at least eight candidates and find a comprehensive set of diagnostic tools to help me choose the one best qualified for sales manager by June 1.

The fourth and last element in each of your Personal Plans is to create written Action Plan Statements for each of the strategies in your Strategies Statement. Action Plans will transform your Strategies from "great ideas" into attained Goals.

Although it is possible to have only one Action Plan for implementing each Strategy, it is more likely that you will need several different Action Plans. Again, because it is important to focus your energies, do not have more than five Action Plans for each of the Strategies you have developed.

Action Plans must satisfy the SMART criteria that we use at The Alternative Board:

Specific
Measurable (impact on Goal attainment)
Attainable
Responsible party
Timeline

The Action Plan Statements for each of your Strategies will demonstrate specific actions. An Action Plan may be brief in content, but it must be specific. It's not enough to merely say, "I will hire a sales trainer." The Action Plan must provide details such as the sales trainer's job description and the resources to be provided such as salary. Action Plans must be measurable and express the results you expect on stated review dates. These measurable results must be reasonably attainable, or the impact will be counterproductive.

Each Action Plan must also specifically name the party responsible for Making It Happen and who needs to be accountable for every task involved in Making It Happen. In most Personal Plans you will be the party responsible, but this will not always be the case. Some plans will involve substantial delegation.

Finally, each Action Plan will state a specific time frame, as well as a schedule for review. Stating that an Action Plan will be reviewed in 30 days is an example of scheduling a time for review. Don't be afraid to look two or three years down the road and then develop progressive Action Plan measurements. Put time-related measurements or benchmark indicators in your Action Plans. The Goal of one man who owned a manufacturing company was to give up his COO responsibilities to someone else within 36 months. One of his Action Plans included hiring the future COO within 6 months, and promoting that person to COO within 36 months. If you have a Goal to lose weight, progressive benchmarks might be losing four pounds by the end of each month during 12 consecutive months.

Action Plan Statement Example

The following is an abstract of part of one business owner's Action Plan Statement that concerned the owner's plan to develop a new product:

- Meet with director of marketing next week. Share plan; get feedback and commitment on type of research needed, as well as reasonableness of 90-day research commitment date. After getting research report from director of marketing, present to planning team at next weekly meeting using a PowerPoint presentation along with handouts outlining the plan.

The Action Plans for each of your Personal Plans should include how you intend to communicate the Action Plan. You will get a lot of ideas on how to execute effective communications in Chapter 4, "The Secret of Results-Driven Communications to Make It Happen."

Now it's your turn to write your Action Plan Statement.

Action Plan Statement Checklist

After you have written your Action Plan Statement, ask yourself the following questions to check and refine your Action Plan Statement:

- Is your Action Plan Statement so clear that there is no question of anyone's misinterpreting its meaning?
- Does your Action Plan Statement have measurements and timelines?
- Will your Action Plan Statement—if achieved—be of major importance in making your Strategies succeed?

Putting It All Together

One year I revised my Personal Vision to include writing books that share some of the Secrets that I and other GEMs use to succeed.

The following excerpt from the Personal Plan I created to achieve this part of my Personal Vision shows how simple it can be to develop a Personal Plan:

CSF: Write and have published books on the following five topics:

- Seven Secrets of GEMs: The GEM Power Formula for Lifelong Success
- The Secrets of GEMs for Starting a Business That Creates Personal and Business Success
- The Secrets of GEMs for Strategic Business Leadership
- The Secrets of GEMs for Winning the Business Financing Game
- The Secrets of GEMs for Succeeding with Family Businesses

Goal: Get a signed contract with a major publisher within 12 months for the Seven Secrets of GEMs and then signed contracts with major publisher(s) for two more books within the next 24 months.

Strategies (the following are two of the five Strategies in my written Strategies Statement for my Goal):

Strategy 1: Sign a contract with a literary agent to represent me for Seven Secrets of GEMs book. The agent must have a proven track record for selling book proposals to major publishing houses.

Strategy 2: Get feedback and additional story contributions on the Seven Secrets manuscript from selected TAB facilitator-coaches who have achieved outstanding success and have helped their members do the same.

Action Plan for Strategy 1:

By January 21: Start work on the table of contents, introduction, and one completed chapter for inclusion in a book proposal draft for Seven Secrets of GEMs and e-mail these items to Lyn by February 6 for editing.

By January 21: Lyn to start work on book proposal and will send me a draft of the completed proposal by March 3.

By March 4: Lyn to research agents that meet my requirements and to send a one-page query letter to prospective agents to find out their level of interest in reading the book proposal for the Seven Secrets of GEMs.

By March 28: Revise and e-mail back to Lyn the book proposal so she can do final editing and then send proposal to each agent who requested it.

By July 1: Talk to agents who have read the book proposal and select agent to represent the book.

Action Plan for Strategy 2:

By March 22: Select 12 of the most successful TAB facilitator-coaches and send out e-mails asking if they will volunteer to review the complete manuscript and contribute additional stories. E-mail must explain my expectations from reviewers.

By April 5: Lyn to send out draft of the complete manuscript to each of the review volunteers requesting their feedback and story contributions before May 1.

By June 22: Revise manuscript based on reviewer feedback and story contributions.

By July 22: Lyn to edit revised manuscript and send me completed draft so it can be sent to agent chosen to represent book.

Every aspect of your Personal Plans will have some level of impact on the relationship you have with your business and/or your family. On the one hand, the books I intend to write will bring greater knowledge to TAB facilitator-coaches, TAB members, and other readers who are not part of the TAB community. On the other hand, the time I will need to devote to these books is time that might have been used for other TAB-related opportunities or enjoying nonbusiness activities.

Now that you understand the four elements involved in creating a Personal Plan, let's look at how others have tied together the four elements of CSFs, Goals, Strategies, and Action Plans to attain their Personal Vision. The following examples explore desires common to many people. They include taking advantage of Competitive Edge Strengths, time away from work, health and recreation, financial freedom, personal development, and personal relationships.

Competitive Edge Strengths

Mieko, who owns a printing company, wrote in his Personal Vision Statement that he desired to spend 75 percent or more of his business time involved in activities directly related to his Competitive Edge Strengths. He felt that it was critical to his happiness at work that he shift the great amount of time he currently spent working on production, which he was great at but did not enjoy doing, to his Competitive Edge Strength of getting new accounts.

Mieko created the following written Personal Plan:

CSF: Focus work time using my competitive edge strength of getting new accounts.

Goal: To be spending a minimum of a third of my time on outside sales within 12 months' time, 60 percent before 24 months' time and a minimum of 75 percent within 36 months' time.

Strategies (the following is one of Mieko's Strategies):

Strategy 1: Hire a production manager.

Action Plan for Strategy 1:

By May 15: Employ a headhunter I have used in the past to find job candidates.

By June 1: Create job description and compensation program for production manager.

July 1: If headhunter has not found a candidate I want to hire, list position in national trade magazines.

No later than August 1: Hire and start training new production manager. I will personally be involved in training for first two months.

By October 1: New hire must be able to run production without my help in time for prime season.

Having a Personal Plan for taking advantage of Competitive Edge Strengths is one of the most essential elements that GEMs use to reach their dreams. This remains true whether you own a business, are thinking about starting a business, work for someone else, or are in college and are trying to figure out what you want to do with your life.

One man, Jerome, had spent a few decades in sales but had never reached great success in this field. One day I was at a planning team meeting in which Jerome's boss, who is president of the company, brought up how poor Jerome's sales results had been for the last year compared to others in his department. The president was mystified by this. He felt that Jerome's winning personality and thorough understanding of what he was selling would make him a guaranteed winner in the selling game.

I asked the president if anyone in the company ever asked Jerome whether he had a passion for his work in sales. The president asked around and found that no one recalled ever having had this discussion with Jerome. The vice president of the company volunteered to discuss the subject with Jerome. The result of their discussion was the confession that despite his many years in sales, Jerome had never enjoyed his job. He was able to do it to a certain level, but he had never truly succeeded because the passion he needed to PAVE the way was missing.

The vice president worked with Jerome to uncover his passions. Within 30 days, Jerome's role in the company was restructured to one in which he was no longer required to close sales, an activity that he dreaded. His new role took advantage of his passion for training and interacting with people. Jerome's career move took him from being an unsuccessful salesperson to being a very important cog in the company's success. What made the difference was passion. It just can't be emphasized enough that without passion there is no Competitive Edge—there is just a built-in formula for stress.

Time Away from Work

One woman, Emilie, who has a successful cosmetics manufacturing business, included in her Personal Vision Statement a desire to play tennis a minimum of three times a week. The following is an excerpt from her Personal Plan:

CSF: Take more time away from the business for tennis by reducing the company's overdependence on me in a way that allows the company to still function and thrive.

Goal: Within 12 months be able to leave the office three times a week to go to tennis club to play a match and partake in the social life of the club.

Strategies (the following is one of Emilie's Strategies):

Strategy 1: Gradually delegate work responsibilities that I do not enjoy to my employees in order to create more open time for tennis.

Action Plan for Strategy 1:

Within one week: Identify the five activities I do at work that I least enjoy and calculate whether the time these combined activities take to accomplish gives me the time I want for tennis.

Within 30 days: Use TAB facilitator-coach to proctor DISC personality profile-behavioral assessment and Wonderlic Personnel Test to all current managers.

Within 30 days of testing: Have TAB facilitator-coach interview managers and provide recommendation of which managers should be delegated which responsibilities.

Within 15 days of recommendations: Actual delegations to take place.

One of the interesting things that came out of Emilie's Action Plans was that the work responsibilities she no longer wanted to have were not turned over to one person. Instead, different portions of the responsibilities were spread out to four different managers. After accomplishing the above Personal Plan, Emilie created another Personal Plan that was very specific to her strategy of becoming a better tennis player.

Having time away from business to spend with family or to use in pursuing personal activities is an aspect found in many business owners' Personal Vision Statements. One of the greatest challenges this vision presents is orchestrating time away from the office that does not negatively impact upon the continual growth of the business. It naturally flows from this that a company must be able to function efficiently without the owner's constant physical presence.

I encourage everyone to have a Personal Plan that deals with recreational pursuits outside of work time. When creating such a Personal Plan, make sure to consider the time allocation you will need for the recreational activity or activities in which you wish to partake. For instance, if one of your Personal Plans involves taking up or spending more time skiing, determine how much time you want to invest in skiing. Is that time realistically available to you? Also consider the expense. For example, when I got involved with trail horses again, I went in knowing how expensive this activity would be. You will not find enjoyment in your recreational pursuits if they drain time you do not have or create overwhelming financial stress.

In small companies overdependence is quite often the major culprit behind owners' being unhappily married to their businesses. The key to reducing this level of dependence is delegating to others those tasks and duties that are not the owner's Competitive Edge Strengths. This becomes easier as a company grows and additional employees are added.

Health

At one point, my Personal Vision Statement included a CSF of low stress. My Goal was to eliminate, within six months time, the pain that occurred in the left side of my neck when I felt stress. One of my Strategies for this Goal was to make meditation a part of my life. One Action Plan for this Strategy called for meditating for 20 minutes twice daily. My stress disappeared within a few months. I followed this routine of meditating from the age of thirty into my early forties.

Meditating required me to make a time commitment that resulted in my not being available for some other activities. To make this work, I had to schedule a specific time each day for meditating during which my family and employees understood that I was not to be disturbed.

You have only a finite amount of time, and it must be managed so that you get the best value from it. One of the benefits of creating written Personal Plans is that doing so helps you better allocate your time. If your Action Plans call for your time to be devoted to certain areas, then quite simply stated, that time is not available to be used for anything else.

Remember Sandy who learned to embrace her natural outgoing behavior after meeting her biological father? Her Personal Vision Statement included having a balanced and healthy lifestyle. Her CSF was to lower her stress level. The Goal for this CSF was to get her blood pressure under control (no more than 130 over 80) within one year.

Sandy reviewed one factor she had written in her Weaknesses Statement:

• The responsibility of being a board member of certain charities is draining my energy, and I feel as though I do not have enough time in the day.

In response to this factor, Sandy created one Strategy to reduce stress by cutting back wherever possible on outside commitments. One of Sandy's Action Plans was to say no to all new outside commitments. The Action Plan included resigning from all charitable boards on which she was a member.

One business owner identified the opportunity to get healthier in his written Opportunities Statement. He took this life opportunity to create a Personal Plan for better health and to improve upon his self-image. The following is an excerpt from his Personal Plan:

CSF: Live healthier.

Goal: Lose 50 pounds within one year.

Strategies (the following are some of his strategies):

Strategy 1: Quit smoking.
Strategy 2: Reduce alcohol consumption.
Strategy 3: Eat better diet.
Strategy 4: Stick to a consistent workout schedule.

Action Plan for Strategy 2:

No more than two drinks of alcohol a day starting immediately.

Financial Freedom

One man, Jonathan, included financial independence as a factor in his Personal Vision Statement. The following outlines some aspects of his Personal Plan:

CSF: Have enough money invested in passive investments to earn sufficient income to allow me to sustain current standard of living.

Goal: Within three years have $500,000 in investments outside the net worth of my home and business.

Strategies (the following is one of his Strategies):

Strategy 1: Invest the maximum amount each month in my 401(k) and make other stock market investments.

Action Plan for Strategy 1:

• Within 30 days, select a financial advisor.

One of my earliest Personal Vision Statements included a desire to accumulate a specific minimum net worth outside of my business ownership assets within 10 years of the day I wrote the factor in my Personal Vision Statement. I identified a CSF of generating a specific minimum net worth from long-term real estate investments. I knew that by investing in income-property real estate, I had some control over the results—unlike the stock market. I went with the investment risk that I was most comfortable taking.

The Goal for my Personal Plan was to buy and rent houses and apartments that would have a market net worth within three years time. The Strategies and Action Plans that went with my Goal were all linked to my personal comfort level. One of my Strategies was to buy houses that needed fix-up work that could be bought with high-financing leverage such as taking over mortgage payments. I could then have the houses repaired and rented.

My Action Plans were very measurable and included details such as how much I wanted to risk in any particular real estate investment and the amount of yearly investments I wanted to make. One Action Plan was to get a real estate broker's license within three months. This would give me easier access to available houses that met my criteria and enable me to buy them more cheaply because of not having to pay the real estate commission. Another Action Plan included lining up bank financing for the purchases within a specific time frame.

Many business owners have told me that they have not invested much of their assets outside their business. As one business owner said, "I've thought about it many times, but I've never invested in a retirement plan because there was always another good use for the money in my business."

Be careful about having too many of your assets tied up in the value of the business you own, or the stock of the company for which you work. Having too many eggs in one basket can be dangerous. I knew one man who had most of his "eggs" in the company stock. The company, which had once been successful, filed for bankruptcy when he was in his mid-fifties, and his stock became worthless. He found himself still working in his sixties at a time when he thought he would be enjoying his retirement.

If investing for the future is not your forte, and for most people it is not, be sure to work with a qualified financial advisor. An advisor will help you accurately project your financial needs for your retirement and show you how to invest wisely.

Personal Development

Remember the business owner who decided to turn his lack of a college degree, which he saw as a weakness, into an opportunity for personal development by getting a college degree while still running his business? He included having a college degree as part of his Personal Vision Statement. The following is an abstract of his Personal Plan:

CSF: Achieve a four-year degree.

Goal: Get a four-year degree within two years of starting classes by attending the college from which I already have accrued credits.

Strategies (the following are some of his Strategies):

Strategy 1: Do not actively try to expand business until I get my degree.

Strategy 2: Budget time between running business and attending college.

Strategy 3: Delegate work that will free up more of my time to focus on getting my degree.

Action Plan: His Action Plans designated the specific amount of time he needed to allocate each week for school and his business, as well as the amount of time he wanted to spend with his wife and children.

Personal Relationships

One business owner declared as a CSF that he wanted to be in a very good marriage or none at all. He set this factor as being critical to the happiness he defined in his Personal Vision Statement. His Goal was very simple: "Have a marriage that brings me happiness within one year or get out of my marriage." It should not come as a surprise to learn that he chose to keep both his CSF and Goal as "Pocket."

One of his Strategies included increasing the time he spent with his wife. One of his Action Plans included signing up for and attending a couples' retreat as well as exploring couples' counseling. Each Action Plan had deadline dates by which it had to take place. His Action Plans also included taking a minimum number of walks a week with his wife and scheduling a steady Tuesday night with his wife for dinner followed by the movies. He also committed to taking a vacation with his wife every few months. His Action Plans included ways to delegate work activities and cut down on business travel so that he could dedicate the time needed to the relationship with his wife. His efforts paid off, and today he is enjoying a happy marriage.

Personal and family relationships require a time commitment to make them work. One of the most frequent comments heard at TAB meetings involves members who bring up complaints made by their spouses because they are not devoting enough time to their families.

This time-commitment factor goes beyond the spousal relationship. One of my time allocations is a commitment to work out with my brother when I go to St. Louis to facilitate my monthly TAB Board meeting. I make sure to factor in the time for us to go to the health club together.

One GEM's Personal Vision stated his desire to spend a lot of quality time with his wife, children, and grandchildren. He also noted wanting more time to spend with several long-term friends whom, because of his having been so focused on building his career, he had not been able to see in a long time. The following is an excerpt from his Personal Plan:

CSF: Allocate more time to nonbusiness relationships.

Goal: Starting immediately, limit my workweek to 45 hours each week unless there is a work crisis that requires more time.

Strategies (the following is one of his Strategies):

Strategy 1: Schedule specific times to spend with both of my long-term male friends.

Action Plan for Strategy 1:

Today: Have assistant call gym and reactivate my membership.

Today: Schedule long lunch every Thursday with friends.

Starting this week: Schedule weekly racquetball games with friends.

It is likely that at some point you will have Personal Plans that directly or indirectly relate to improving your personal relationships whether in your marriage or with your family or close friends. These are all seemingly simple aspirations that sadly are much more difficult to attain when work pulls you into its vortex. GEMs are masters at creating and implementing Personal Plans that provide a balance between life and work. You will find that creating a Personal Plan for such a balance is likely to be among your earliest of Personal Plans.

One mergers-and-acquisitions specialist found his marriage suffering due to his constant travel and time away from home. His Personal Plan included devoting more time to his marriage.

The following is an abstract of his Personal Plan:

CSF: Partake in activity with wife that we both enjoy doing.

Goal: Within three months' time begin attending ballroom dance activities with my wife two nights a week.

Strategies (the following is one of his Strategies):

Strategy 1: Reduce all business-related travel so that I am home by Thursday night of each week.

Action Plan for Strategy 1:

Within one week: Call key accounts and communicate my Goal in order to secure their cooperation in scheduling meeting times.

Immediately: Notify my assistant that she is to stop scheduling me for any travel between Thursday and Sunday unless it is for a trade show or other event at which I am specifically needed to be present as the owner of the company.

Immediately: Find someone to take my place in attending trade shows with salespeople because shows generally include weekends.

His Goal was reached well within the 12-month time limit he set.

Needs of the Psyche

One business owner took enormous pleasure in public speaking and was quite skilled at it. There was also a psychic factor involved as the business owner had never forgotten the incredible high he got upon winning a college intramural speaking contest years earlier. He wanted to find a regular way to revisit that satisfying high, and he wanted the personal and business recognition that he felt was attainable if he could have speaking engagements and handle media relations on topics involving his industry.

The following is an excerpt from his Personal Plan:

CSF: Become recognized as a leading expert speaker to the industry.

Goal: Secure five speaking engagements before local or national industry trade associations within next 18 months.

Strategies:

Strategy 1: Create a PowerPoint presentation and script for a talk that is of interest to the industry.

Strategy 2: Register with speaking brokers.

Strategy 3: Create marketing materials including a preview tape for potential speaking engagements.

Strategy 4: Hire media relations agent.

Strategy 5: Contact local chapters of trade organizations throughout United States to offer free speaking services.

Action Plan for Strategy 1:

Within 30 days: Dictate and edit 15 double-spaced pages to use as a script for a talk to be offered.

Within 30 days of a completed script: Create a 20-slide PowerPoint presentation for my talk.

Within 90 days of creating PowerPoint presentation: Give a talk before a group and modify the talk to enhance it based on this speaking experience.

What are your psychic needs that will bring greater fulfillment to your life? Perhaps you want to be well recognized in your trade association, or you have a desire for your company to be number 1 in its industry. Many business owners have the psychic need to appear in television commercials for their companies. Don't undervalue or judge your psychic needs when developing your Personal Plans.

Challenging Your Personal Plans

TAB facilitator-coach Barba Hickman shared with me a story about one TAB member who presented a draft of a Personal Plan to his fellow TAB Board members. His plan included hiring a salesperson who would assume a large portion of the selling responsibilities that up to that point had been held solely by the member. The member had found a candidate he liked, but the candidate wanted the title of vice president of sales.

Several members of the TAB Board challenged his Personal Plan and expressed their views that it would be a mistake to give the title of vice president of sales to the first salesperson hired. Certain members shared their experiences of having made that mistake in the past. One member recalled how in giving his first salesperson the title of vice president of sales, he had also given that salesperson "nowhere to go but down." The member further explained that the second salesperson he hired was far more talented, but he had already given the vice president title away.

The Board members discussed the fact that it would be best if the new salesperson could be hired with the title of sales representative. But if the candidate was adamant about wanting a more impressive title, the new employee could be started with the title of director of sales. This way when an expanded sales staff was needed, the member would have the opportunity to decide whether the first salesperson was the right person to lead the department or whether a different person should have the title of vice president. The challenges provided by the TAB Board resulted in changes to the member's Personal Plan that reflected the good advice he had obtained.

One of the benefits TAB members receive from sharing the drafts of their Personal Plans with their fellow TAB Board members and their TAB facilitator-coaches is that it gives them a forum for unbiased challenges. Often the mere process of having Personal Plans challenged results in a major reemphasis or redirection of the plans that have a dramatic positive impact.

To the extent that you feel comfortable, share the drafts of your Personal Plans with trusted advisors. I don't want to give the impression that you cannot start putting a Personal Plan into action without first getting advice, but your Personal Plan will benefit from the challenges you may receive from others. Additionally, if your Personal Plan is validated by those you trust and respect, that validation will provide you with additional confidence.

Eliminating Personal Plans

One of the Personal Plans I had during the early years of TAB was to start a monthly newsletter for entrepreneurs by entrepreneurs. At first I wrote all the articles for the newsletter *Tips from the Top* myself. I continued to write all the articles for the newsletter until I started getting contributions of tips and advice from TAB members and TAB franchisee facilitator-coaches. As the number of tips and the amount of advice that were contributed by others grew, my role decreased to the point that I was writing only a single, monthly article. I had reached my Goal with the newsletter, and so I eliminated that Personal Plan and added another.

Hopefully the Goals in each of your Personal Plans will be reached, and as this takes place, you will be eliminating these plans. Remember, your Personal Plans are not meant to be permanent or long term. In Chapter 7, "The Secret of Changing Course," you will learn the process of eliminating Personal Plans and adding new Personal Plans.

CHAPTER 4

THE SECRET OF
RESULTS-DRIVEN COMMUNICATIONS TO MAKE IT HAPPEN

Many business owners have plans, even great plans, but they fail when it comes to making them happen. One of the key reasons this happens is due to inefficient communications. Business owners and managers typically tread water in the area of communications. They may, in their own frazzled perception, believe they are in touch with their employees, clients, family, and friends, but all too often these needed lines of communication do not exist.

In contrast, GEMs use Results-Driven Communications to generate the power they need to infuse their employees, family, friends, and themselves with the passion needed to make their plans happen. This chapter on Results-Driven Communications will help you to transform your life, relationships, and business because it provides a comprehensive, refreshingly real, and practical approach to bringing about the life of fulfillment and happiness you desire.

There are three steps to achieving Results-Driven Communications. The first step is to build trusting two-way communications, and this chapter gives you six methods for doing that. The second step is to determine what the best communication tool is for the situation at hand and use it to your maximum advantage. This chapter gives you five tools that GEMs use to make their communications as successful as possible. The third step is to smash through communication barriers that can prevent you from getting what you need. This chapter describes four barriers that commonly arise to successful communications and how to smash through them.

Step 1: Build Trusting Two-Way Communications

Building trusting two-way communications is an essential step in developing the Results-Driven Communications you need to make your Personal Plans happen. Without establishing and maintaining open communication lines with those who are critical to making your Personal Plans happen, Results-Driven Communications are simply not possible.

GEMs know that trusting two-way communication greatly enhances the cooperation they receive from others in making their Personal Plans happen. Too many business owners mistakenly assume that being the boss automatically creates a situation in which their employees will do whatever it takes to give them the results they want. GEMs know that the effectiveness of one-way communication is short lived at best.

GEMs take the time to establish the foundation of two-way trust by creating an atmosphere that encourages open two-way communications. Once two-way communication is established, they nurture and encourage the two-way trust that has developed so that it continually fosters enthusiasm in others and ensures that everyone involved in making the GEMs' Personal Plans happen truly want to give their best efforts. Let's take a look at the methods GEMs use to establish two-way trust and how this leads to making their Personal Plans happen.

Building Trusting Two-Way Communications Method 1: Applying TABenos

At The Alternative Board we coach our members, who are business owners, to use a technique called "TABenos" to create open and trusting two-way communications. *TABenos* is derived from the ancient Greek word *temenos*, which is translated as "sanctuary." TABenos involves a series of exercises that minimizes the natural defenses people have to open communications by creating a safe space or sanctuary that is conducive to communications.

The TABenos exercise series evolved with its use over the years. The exercises consist of asking the group involved—whether that be a management team or your family or some other group—three simple questions. The responses must be written as they are given, and there should be no judgment on the responses as to whether they are right or wrong. I prefer that the responses to these questions be written down on a board or a large pad of paper displayed on an easel so that everyone involved can easily read them.

The first question asks participants to identify what their protective armor or communication defenses look like. The second question asks what actions taken by others cause them to don this armor. The last question asks what benefits will be gained as a result of feeling safe to set aside this armor in order to conduct the meeting within a safe and open TABenos environment.

One of the keys to keeping the environment safe for open communications is having all the participants make the commitment that in future meetings they will refrain from making any of the comments or actions identified to cause others to don their armor. If, despite this commitment, a violation of the agreement is made, the other participants may confront the person who made the violation. Only when all those participating in the exercise refrain from comments or actions that cause others to don armor can there be a true TABenos meeting environment.

The TABenos list developed by one company's planning team noted that using the term "stupid" to refer to an action or comment by another team member was a major cause for armor to be donned and for open communications to shut down. At the very next meeting, one of the members referred to an idea being expressed as "stupid." Another member immediately pointed out the commitment that the group had made to not using the term "stupid." Over a year later the owner of the company commented to me that he was amazed at how quickly the cooperation among his management team had improved from the moment attention was called to this violation of the TABenos contract.

The following are excerpts from the results of the TABenos exercises as they were answered by the TAB planning team:

List 1: Displays of Armor or Defense Mechanisms
- Interrupting
- Sabotaging
- Responding defensively
- Deflecting and/or changing the subject
- Avoiding or bypassing the issue
- Yelling
- Being sarcastic; making cynical remarks
- Rolling the eyes
- Sighing

List 2: Causes of Armor or Defense Mechanisms to Appear
- Having side conversations
- Being overly aggressive
- Attempting to control
- Appearing to treat some people with favoritism
- Withholding facts
- Being overly emotional
- Not listening

- Grandstanding, overselling, and/or persuading
- Making excuses
- Devaluing others' opinions based on their years and/or experience

List 3: Benefits of Reducing Armor
- Greater participation
- Enhanced teamwork
- Greater productivity
- Better preparation
- Increased creativity
- Better use of time and energy, thereby increasing effectiveness
- Synergistic solutions
- Accountability
- Trust
- Motivation

Bill Vrettos, a TAB facilitator-coach in Grand Junction, Colorado, applies the principles of TABenos at home with his family. Vrettos told me, "At holidays, I place a bucket by the front door, and all family members are required to symbolically leave their armor in the bucket as they enter. When there is no fear of personal attack and defenses are laid to rest, we can fully enjoy an enriching family atmosphere."

The following are some of the responses from Vrettos's family concerning what their armor looks like and the benefits of eliminating the defenses to open communications.

The Vrettos Clan
Q: What does your armor look like?
A: • Sarcasm
- Projecting our feelings onto others
- Distrust

- Not listening
- Defensiveness
- Aggression
- Anger
- Withdrawal from communication
- Becoming overly talkative

Q: What do we have to gain as a family by eliminating the armor that exists within our family communications?

A: • We would have a genuine exchange of information and feelings.
- We would know how others in the family are feeling.
- We would be more productive.
- We would feel safe, secure, and comfortable.
- We would understand why others are acting the way they are.
- We would have a source for renewing our spiritual ties.
- We would have a "safe port" in the storm of life.

TABenos helps to eliminate the resistance of communication defenses that are part of the personal armor of those whose help you need to effect your Personal Plans. The TABenos methodology works equally well in keeping communication lines open in both business and nonbusiness situations.

Building Trusting Two-Way Communications Method 2: Discussing Plans Openly

Early in the existence of The Alternative Board, I noticed several weaknesses that started to develop as the company began to grow. I called upon certain TAB executives, whose input on the situation I felt could be especially valuable, to meet with me. At the meeting I detailed my observations of the weaknesses and shared my thoughts about the possible corrections that needed to take place. Then I opened up the floor to the thoughts and ideas of the executives I had called into the meeting. When the meeting was over, one of the executives thanked me for trusting him enough to involve him in such an important matter.

By meeting with these employees, I conveyed to them that I trusted and valued their thoughts and ideas. By being open with them, I helped to establish a core understanding that they could trust that I would be open with them and that I trusted they would be open with me in return.

For most business owners the types of things that I openly discussed with the executives at the meeting mentioned above would have remained as Pocket elements of their plans. The tendency for most business owners is to not discuss these types of situations with any of their executives or employees. Instead, they typically make a decision and then demand that their employees meet the expected results with no questions asked. Because the typical entrepreneurial nature is to just "get things done," too many of their plans are kept private and in their Pocket.

One of the Results-Driven Communications ground rules is telling those who are critical to making your Personal Plans happen as much as possible regarding what you are trying to accomplish and why. If the people who are critical to making your Personal Plans happen don't understand or know what you require of them or what your desired outcome is, they cannot maximize their effectiveness in helping you accomplish your goals. The more information you share, the greater the level of two-way trust you will establish. The more knowledge your people have, the greater their buy-in will be to your Personal Plans and the more motivated they will be to provide help.

Remember Jim, the bakery owner who had a weakness in detail and operational responsibilities? He openly shared most aspects (as they related to his business) of his Personal Vision, SWOT analysis, and Personal Plans with his managers. Communicating his Weaknesses Statement allowed his managers to gain an under-standing of why Jim needed to delegate certain responsibilities in which he was weak and helped them buy in to his Personal Plans to offset his weaknesses. One of the reasons behind the great suc-cess of Jim's company was the trusting two-way communications that he established by sharing so many aspects of his personal written statements.

What level of trusting two-way communications exists between you and the employees, family, friends, and others who are critical to making your Personal Plans happen? If participants who are crucial to making your Personal Plans happen are oper-ating with only part of the knowledge of what you really want, it is unlikely that you will be able to access their full cooperation in maximizing your success. To the extent that you feel comfort-able, communicate the Critical Success Factors, Goals, Strategies, and Action Plans that affect those whose help you require.

Without a doubt there will be plans or aspects of plans that you choose to keep in your Pocket and to share with no one at all. There will also be times that you delay giving details about the total picture of certain plans and provide others with only partial details. During the months that Jason and I discussed the possibility of his joining The Alternative Board as COO, I did not mention these discussions to any TAB employees. I did tell them that I was going to hire a new COO for TAB. However, I felt that I should not communicate the full details until after Jason made a firm commitment to join The Alternative Board. When he decided to join TAB, I promptly informed the employees of the decision.

Ask yourself if those whose participation is required in mak-ing your Personal Plans happen could give you greater support if they had more information about your plans. GEMs who have companies with layers of employees typically share needed infor-mation concerning their plans in stages. They first determine those who can provide valuable feedback that may result in possible modifications to their plans. After receiving this feedback and making any needed modifications, they go on to share their plans with other levels of employees who are involved with or affected by the plans.

Before I discuss my Personal Plans involving TAB with anyone in the company, I first discuss them with Jason. As a result of our discussions, I often modify my plans. Only then do I take the plans further out of Pocket and discuss them with the TAB planning team. There are times that my plans are communicated no further than the TAB planning team and other times when information about my plans may get shared with a specific department or even with all TAB employees.

Another factor that will affect the level of trusting two-way communications in your company is your employees' perception of whether you really want, rather than just say you want, open communications. One business owner enlisted my help to find out why sales and profits for his company plans had not been met. For three straight years the numbers had dropped sharply despite what the owner considered outstanding management, highly competitive pricing, and state-of-the-art technology.

After speaking to several of his employees, I learned that the products the owner felt were state of the art were, in fact, sadly behind the times. His employees did not feel safe to express their views to the owner, nor did they challenge such things as the products being "state of the art" because they saw the owner as being someone who went blissfully along wearing "status quo blinders." His employees were convinced that he did not want to know the truth, and they feared that any such honesty might cost them their jobs.

The owner was disturbed when I relayed his employees' comments to him. He told me that what shocked him the most was finding out that his employees did not feel safe to let him know how they felt. The problem was that trusting two-way communications were not established between the owner and his employees.

It is not enough to say what you expect from your employees relating to trust and what, in turn, they should expect from you. Establishing a true sense of trusting two-way communications comes from showing that you trust your employees through actions that say, "I want and need your input and your efforts."

Building Trusting Two-Way Communications Method 3: Adapting Your Communication Style to the Personality Needs of Others

One executive who was a key factor in making many of my plans succeed was perceived by his coworkers as having a strong air of overconfidence and of being condescending. Surprisingly, despite the perception others had of him, I found that even the slightest hint of criticism thrown his way caused him to lose focus and become overly defensive. As soon as he heard me say anything that he interpreted as criticism, his facial expressions and body language clearly changed to indicate that his focus on what we were discussing was lost and that he was instead thinking about how he was going to verbally deflect the perceived criticism.

I had a heart-to-heart chat with him about these issues. He said the problem stemmed from his childhood and that his air of over-confidence was in truth a cover for his low self-esteem. This also explained why he was so sensitive to perceived criticism. I had to decide what communication style would be most effective to use with this executive so that he would not feel threatened and lose his focus.

I needed to establish trusting two-way communications with the executive. So, from that point on, whenever he was doing things wrong, I always tried to begin my communications with him by mentioning something that he was doing right (and he did most things right). Then I would talk to him about the things he was doing that did not satisfy me. I criticized his actions but not him as a person. After I began using a communication style that was tailored to his personality, the barriers to our trusting two-way communications mostly went away. His self-esteem issues very rarely got in the way of his efforts to make my plans happen.

People have unique and consistent personality traits that define them. GEMs know that it is far easier to adjust or adapt their communication techniques to the personality needs of others than it is to change the people with whom they interact. Take the time to identify the specific personality traits of those whose help you need in making your Personal Plans happen. Ask yourself what communication style is most effective for creating trusting two-way communications with the person based on the personality or behavior style of the person with whom you need to communicate. Then make a consistent effort to use that style of communication whenever you are dealing with that person.

Building Trusting Two-Way Communications Method 4: Maintaining an Atmosphere That Is Open for Communications

Choosing the proper place to conduct your communications is one of the atmosphere factors that can go a long way in establishing trusting two-way communications. Choose the location for your communications based on the purpose of the meeting and the person or group of people to whom you need to communicate. When you are trying to establishing trusting two-way communications, meeting in a nonintimidating location can be a big help.

When I was president at Tipton, I would occasionally meet with small groups of employees outside the company premises. At times I went to local hangouts that were frequented by some of the employees. I would buy a round of drinks and talk a bit of shop. This allowed the workers to gain a deeper understanding of what the dreams and philosophy of the company were and to tell me their views on plans that directly involved them.

During these meetings, trusting two-way communications were established and reinforced with some employees who might never have opened up in a formal setting at the office. The unspoken rule was that, during that time and in that space, employees could ask me questions or make comments about anything and there would be no repercussions. Many times I learned more from these casual discussions than I did in lengthy talks with company managers.

Off-premises interaction with groups of employees is a great way to create an atmosphere where employees feel more comfortable. This type of atmosphere will help you gain open communications from your workers. This might range from eating meals out together to camping out. The key is to remove the barrier to trusting two-way communications that sometimes exists because of the physical setting by creating a very informal, non-threatening atmosphere.

The number of people you include in a meeting can also greatly impact the level of openness in the communication you wish to conduct. A very large group is often an ineffective forum for establishing trusting two-way communications. Often people will be more open and trusting with others who are part of a common group such as employees in a single department or store than they will be if they are in a group meeting with others with whom they do not feel as close.

Building Trusting Two-Way Communications Method 5: Being Clear about Accountability

The owner of a drug-packaging firm had a foreman who was the kind of employee any manager would want—as long as things were going smoothly. Whenever objectives set forth in written Action Plans to which the foreman had agreed to be accountable were not met, the foreman would put up a smoke screen a mile long. He seemed to think that a problem would go away if he talked fast and loud about it not being "his" fault while rushing about in a huff trying to find someone among his subordinates on whom to pin the blame. Things came to a head one day when the owner overheard that one of his employees had brought down the house in the employee cafeteria by doing an animated imitation of the manager denying anything was his fault.

The owner met with the manager and explained that if he was unwilling or unable to accept responsibility for results that he had clearly agreed to achieve in written Action Plans, he would be removed from his position. Thereafter the manager vocalized his concerns if he felt that objectives were unreasonable to achieve and committed only to actions that he felt were reasonably attainable. Because the owner confronted him about his accountability expectations using a head-on communications approach, the manager became someone who accepted accountability and achieved what he had committed to achieving.

GEMs meet potential conflicts and difficult situations, including dealing with difficult people, by communicating head-on. In contrast, too many business owners do not clearly communicate in a head-on manner the expectations they have for those responsible for making their plans happen. The best way to give a clear message of accountability is to be direct and address the problem as soon as you see that the employee is not accepting responsibility. Personal Plans that are dependent on company results will not be achieved unless all employees involved accept responsibility to get results in a timely manner for whatever is required of them in the Action Plans.

Trusting two-way communications require that others know where they stand with you at all times. Employees should know that you meet conflicts head-on so they don't have to be concerned that you are holding back on your feelings and expectations. It is better to make people aware of your feelings early in the game if you see that they are not accepting accountability rather than letting the matter get to a boiling point. When you avoid directly confronting a person who is not accepting responsibility, you are communicating that you accept their lack of accountability.

Remember the business owner who gave a raise to his assistant even though she was hurting his productivity? His avoidance of head-on communications was a definite weakness that prevented him from achieving his Personal Plans. Caving in to difficult personalities and situations by sticking your head in the sand and hoping that the conflict will go away is a sure way to sabotage your Personal Plans.

Some employees will use every method imaginable, and some you may not have imagined, to avoid taking responsibility for poor results unless there is a clear message of accountability made by the business owner. The "blameless" employee can be found at every level of those businesses that are underachieving. While such employees are busy avoiding blame, they are also eroding the productivity and morale of those who work around them.

One business owner told me that his company missed its sales goal projection because it was experiencing a poor on-time delivery record that was resulting in lost customers. He explained that the situation existed because his management team considered the poor delivery record acceptable. I pointed out to the business owner that he was responsible for the corporate culture that had allowed his managers to not keep commitments without any repercussions. The members of his management team were obviously not going to do anything to change the situation as long they could get away with it.

He needed to get across a big message regarding his expectations of employee accountability. I suggested he start by distributing a memo to his department heads that made it clear that as of January 1 of the following year, quarterly bonuses would not be paid to any manager who committed to time-dependent completion dates if the dates were not met. Even with the memo it took some time before his managers realized the owner would no longer let them slide on their commitments. The owner didn't succeed in keeping all the managers accountable to the company culture until he actually withheld bonuses from those who didn't meet their commitments.

Building Trusting Two-Way Communications Method 6: Keeping Your Emotions in Check

TAB facilitator-coach Barba Hickman has one member who asked her to talk to his employees in order to help him uncover why he had such a large employee-turnover problem. The member told her that he thought that the problem existed because similar companies in the area were paying higher wages but that he was not sure this was the only reason.

In speaking to the top employees of the member, Hickman found that the business owner had no idea that the reason his employees were leaving was because there was an absolute lack of trusting two-way communications. While the employees were highly loyal to one another, they openly admitted that they did not feel this way about their boss.

The employees related to Hickman that her member, who appeared to be very mild mannered at TAB meetings and coaching sessions, was apparently not mild mannered with his employees. His impatience often resulted in his publicly "exploding." Employees were leaving the company because they had become tired of the highly charged, unfair atmosphere he created with his "verbal explosions."

Learning the reasons that were responsible for his employee-turnover problem brought about a major effort on the part of the TAB member to avoid emotional responses when he was upset. He held back from taking part in potentially emotional communications until he felt he was able to discuss things calmly.

Allowing yourself to be overcome by emotions, especially when it results in yelling or hostile behavior during a meeting, will be counterproductive to establishing and maintaining trusting two-way communications. The general counsel of one company left the company because he said that the business owner yelled at him one day after discovering that he had not sent out documents that were needed for a particular deal. The business owner, who had a common physical manifestation of raising his voice to a higher volume when he was frustrated, did not recall yelling at the general counsel.

If you have a habit of raising your voice when you are frustrated or upset, make a conscious effort to lower the volume of your voice when this starts to happen. In addition to helping you keep your emotions under control, lowering your voice will force the other party or parties you are dealing with to pay closer attention to what you have to say.

I once witnessed a situation in a meeting in which an employee disagreed with the business owner on the value of a marketing approach the company had been using. The response by the owner to the group was that the employee did not know what he was talking about. This destroyed the kind of meeting atmosphere the business owner wanted.

How you respond to suggestions that are given in a public setting will greatly affect the desired meeting atmosphere and development of trusting two-way communications. If part of your communication involves a negative reaction to a comment of a particular person, be careful how you express it. If you are not sensitive to this, that person, as well as the others in the group who witness the exchange, may withhold valuable feedback in the future.

Very few people are receptive to public criticism. If you have ever been criticized in public, you probably took it personally and resented the person who criticized you. Public criticism can destroy the kind of trusting two-way communications you want.

If your emotions are getting out of hand during a meeting and you feel that you cannot control them, close the meeting and reschedule it for another time when you are in better control of your emotions. If you continue with a meeting when you are even teetering on losing your cool, you may say something you regret and that you cannot undo.

Taking even a temporary time-out to reduce your stress level can result in reopening a meeting with a totally different emotional tone and atmosphere. I have used temporary, half-hour time-outs to meditate and bring my stress level down before continuing with meetings. A short time-out gives me the opportunity to bring about a different mindset with greater focus on whatever is bothering me. During the time-out I may come up with alternatives that were not on the table, in part, because the stress levels at the meeting were too high.

Step 2: Use Results-Driven Communications Tools

GEMs take the time to identify and use the communications tools that will make their communications more successful. Using the right communications tools in a particular situation will bring about a sense of clarity for those whose help you need in making your Personal Plans happen. GEMs take the time to identify and then use the communications tools that will be most effective in generating excitement for each of their Personal Plans.

Let's take a look at some of the tools GEMs use to make their communications more powerful.

Communications Tool 1: The Written Culture Statement

One manufacturer told me that a culture had evolved in his company that he described as an "I never make mistakes" attitude. This unwanted culture was a key factor in preventing his Personal Plans, as they were impacted by his company, from succeeding. He embarked upon eliminating the I-never-make-mistakes attitude within his company by issuing a written company Culture

Statement that made it clear that employees were expected to admit their mistakes and to not make excuses.

A written Culture Statement is a communications tool that GEMs use for bringing about a company culture that helps to make their plans happen. It is not uncommon for business owners to fail in getting the results they desire when key executives have a vastly different style of management and values than they do. Culture has a tendency to evolve erratically and on its own unless addressed specifically by the business owner. Without a written Culture Statement, culture among employees can directly clash with the unspoken values of the owner.

Develop a written Culture Statement, and distribute it to all your current employees and to those whom you are thinking about hiring. The written Culture Statements of companies owned by GEMs include such things as the core values of how employees are to be treated as well as the way employees are expected to interact with customers, clients, and others who are important to the company. The desired culture also specifically states such things as the owner's expectations of accountability.

One business owner's Personal Plan for reducing the stress in life included changing his company's culture. His Personal Plan is provided, in part, as follows:

CSF: Keep stress at work and away from work to a minimum.

Goal: Reduce blood pressure to no more than 130 over 80 within six months.

Strategy 1: Change company culture to one that involves a less stressful environment.

> **One of the additional benefits of creating a companywide culture that matches your belief system is that it will go a long way in helping you keep your stress level to a minimum.**

Action Plan for Strategy 1:

By June 1: Write and distribute written company Culture Statement.

By August 1: Replace executive X with one who shares the culture I desire for the company.

By December 1: Identify any executives who continue to work against my desired company culture and make plans to replace them if the resistance continues after giving a 30-day warning.

It took two years to get the culture completely in line with the owner's values.

Early in the history of The Alternative Board, I greatly reduced my involvement with the company for a four-year period because of a decision I made to spend time with a specific family member. During this time period major cultural changes took place at TAB. When I once again increased my involvement in the company, I realized that the cultural changes were directly responsible for certain plans failing to be achieved.

I developed a Personal Plan for changing the company culture back to one that was consistent with what I wanted. As part of the plan, I wrote a TAB Culture Statement and sent a copy of this statement to all employees of TAB. This TAB Culture Statement, along with actions to back it up, helped return the company culture to the results-oriented culture consistent with my Personal Vision.

At The Alternative Board we always give a copy of our written Culture Statement to any potential employees whom TAB interviews. The statement explains that prospective employees of TAB—as with any persons considering employment by any privately owned business—should first understand the controlling owner's desires for the overall culture of the business. Before joining the TAB community, prospective employees need to determine whether this culture is compatible with the work environment they require for being happy and productive in their own career goals.

The following are some of the other essential factors expressed in the TAB Culture Statement that has helped make our plans happen:

- Employees must keep their word, be truthful, and not mislead anyone or misrepresent anything.
- We will succeed as a team. This requires direct communication that embraces respect and is without hidden political agendas. One of the advantages of working for a privately owned business is that one's career path can be successful without the politics that are highly prevalent in publicly owned companies.
- When an employee is wrong, the employee is expected to acknowledge that he or she is wrong rather than making excuses.
- Employees must keep all internal confidences. Discovery of any information of a confidential basis that is found to have been given by a TAB employee to a person not authorized to receive this information will be grounds for immediate dismissal.

Communications Tool 2: The Agenda

I once sat in on a meeting of store managers that was called by a business owner of a retail chain to discuss an exciting expansion plan for the company. The business owner opened the meeting by speaking for 30 minutes about miscellaneous things before he finally got around to discussing the plan about which the meeting had been called. As he rambled on, you could see some of the store managers fighting to keep their eyes open. By the time he got around to presenting the plan and requesting feedback on it from the store managers, he had lost their interest.

The business owner should have developed a written agenda for the meeting and followed it. This would have kept the meeting on target and prevented it from going off on tangents that took away from the primary focus of the meeting.

A written agenda is an essential tool that you can use for any meeting. The act of preparing the agenda will in itself force you to think about the main points you are trying to communicate. An agenda will also help you emphasize positive matters such as potential impact on the growth of the company and point out major areas where you have concern.

Decide in advance roughly how much time is needed for communicating each point on your agenda, and then present your points in a concise manner that keeps to your time schedule. Be sure to include a question-and-answer time for each major point to reaffirm that your communications have been fully understood by all in attendance at the meeting.

Communications Tool 3: The Letter to Employees' Family Members

At Tipton we kept the immediate family members of all our salespeople informed about the ongoing status of leading salespeople in our company sales contests. This brought about family motivation for the salespeople to achieve greater success. The night of one award dinner, the wife of a salesman who was awarded a cruise to the Caribbean told me, "I should get full credit for this because I am the one who pushed him to win the contest."

Ask yourself if there are people who, while they may not be essential to making your plans take place, can still provide help to Make It Happen. Gaining the support of your employees' family members often provides great benefit in making your Personal Plans happen. The family members of your employees can greatly affect the morale and effort of your employees. In the same way, negative feelings generated by family members can contribute to the negative attitude of your employees.

Consider sharing some exciting portion of your plans that involve the company with the family members of your employees as a method of getting family members emotionally involved in some positive aspect of the plans. One GEM sends a letter to the home of every one of his 100-plus employees every calendar quarter. The letter notes the achievements of various groups and individuals and always includes the owner's Personal Vision for the future of the company.

Communications Tool 4: The Visual Aids

The expression "One picture is worth a thousand words" is certainly true when it come to presenting your Personal Plans. Visual aids help give a clearer picture of what you are presenting and can help break up the monotony that words alone can create.

Visual aid tools for Results-Driven Communications include things such as PowerPoint presentations and Webcasts. If you are trying to get across the sales results projected for the next few years, showing a graph via a PowerPoint presentation will provide additional reinforcement to your message. A graph demonstrating growth patterns can be a lot more dramatic than oral statements.

Communications Tool 5: The Written Backup

When I first started communicating aspects of my Personal Plans to those who would be helping me to make them happen, I did so face-to-face or over the telephone in order to save time. The problem with this method was that the same words meant different things to different people. Too often what I said was not received with the proper understanding of the information I was trying to convey.

While you will likely make the initial communication of your Personal Plans in person, it is important to back up what you have said in writing. Communicating your Personal Plans in writing will nip miscommunication problems in the bud when they are still small—before misunderstandings get to a point where they disrupt, or even destroy, the chances of success for your Personal Plans.

Often when a plan is discussed orally, and without written backup, the parties involved are left with different impressions of exactly what was said and what is wanted. By describing in detail, in an e-mail or memo, exactly what your expectations are, or sending a written record to clarify what was discussed, there should be no miscommunication of what is being requested or desired.

At one point I saw a need to develop an advance training program for the facilitator-coaches of The Alternative Board. I had a survey conducted to identify the business areas in which TAB members most needed additional knowledge for themselves and for helping their members. I communicated my Personal Plan for this endeavor to key executives at TAB via a two-phase process. First I sent an e-mail. Then I followed up the e-mail with a group meeting during which the executives received a written copy of my Personal Plan for the advance training program, which we then discussed and revised.

Step 3: Smash the Communications Barriers

Sometimes in order to get things done, you need to smash through the communications barriers that are keeping you from reaching the level of success and happiness you desire. GEMs smash through traditionally accepted rules of communications and make their own rules. They know that they need to do whatever it takes to establish Results-Driven Communications. GEMs are not constrained by their egos or a need for recognition when they communicate, nor do they worry about political ramifications as is often the case in publicly held companies. They simply communicate in whatever way is needed to get the results they want.

Communications Barrier 1: Not Communicating Directly with Nondirect Reports

The Alternative Board has a Web-based library where TAB members can access tips and advice from others in the TAB Community. When I want something researched in the TAB library, I may contact the head of marketing and ask if the marketing intern can do the research for me. The head of marketing knows that I expect her to tell me if this will interfere with other assignments she has given the intern. But in the interest of saving time, it is just as likely that I will call the intern directly with the request and ask her to check with her supervisor to see if she can manage the work I have requested.

In theory taught in college management programs, the CEO never bypasses direct reports to manage or request things from subordinates. In reality, every GEM at some time or another bypasses direct reports to manage or request things from the subordinates of those who directly report to them. They also use this approach to get feedback that they feel they are not getting by going through the normal channels. The key is to understand how to communicate the bypassing request without being disruptive.

At The Alternative Board this approach to communications is explained as follows in the written TAB Company Culture Statement:

> As the controlling owner of TAB, Allen Fishman will not restrict his involvement solely to those executives reporting directly to him but will interact with TAB employees of all levels. Because Allen Fishman is often not physically at the TAB Headquarters, this interaction will often take place via e-mail or telephone calls. Allen will always assume that

whatever projects or assignments he gives will be treated with the highest degree of priority, unless he specifically states that it is not high priority. If this creates a conflict with other assignments you may have, it is imperative that you discuss this with your department head who will work out the priorities directly with Allen Fishman.

When GEMs bypass direct reports, they may inform the parties to whom the subordinates report, but generally they do not ask for their permission. When possible, you should check with the person to whom the subordinate reports so that your request will not conflict with any projects or assignments already given to the subordinate. However, it is more likely that you will ask the employee to check with his or her supervisor.

Just because projects come from the business owner does not mean that they are necessarily more important than projects assigned by others. However, in the real world, employees will treat projects from the boss as a priority in order to make the business owner happy—unless another prioritization is given to the subordinate.

In contrast, in a publicly owned company, the CEO would typically go through a chain of command by first stating his request to the level below him who then might request it from the level below him and so on. A single request is likely to go through several levels of communications before arriving at the employee who will actually execute the request. This communications bypass difference is one of the operational advantages that exist for privately owned businesses in making things happen more efficiently.

Communications Barrier 2: Not Announcing Expected Accomplishments to Avoid Putting Pressure on Yourself

In the early years of TAB, I announced my membership goals for the company. I used this announcement, in part, to put additional pressure on myself and the others who were working on this project so that we would reach our membership goals on time. I have always used communications to motivate myself and others.

When I was preparing to take the California Bar exam, I told my associates that I would pass the bar on the first attempt. I did this to invoke additional motivation to study. There were nights when I asked myself, "Should I study or go out?" The fear of embarrassment if I failed after I had made it very clear to people that I was going to pass the bar the first time was a major factor in motivating me to study.

Traditional rules of business communications would state that you should never announce expected accomplishments to create pressure for yourself. GEMs defy these traditional rules and often create self-motivation by announcing expected accomplishments. It is undeniable that there is a self-motivational power involved in announcing an intended sales increase for a company or declaring the timing of a new product that helps get results. I recommend that you apply this technique only to very important matters. You don't want to put this level of pressure on yourself on a day-to-day basis.

Another way to use self-motivation communications is to communicate to your family, employees, or friends some special reward for when you have accomplished something you have set out to achieve. Think up a reward that is over and above the accomplishment itself, something that will really excite the others around you.

Early in my business career I set up a reward of taking several of my family members and friends to a special restaurant in a chauffeur-driven limousine upon the completion of a transaction that I had worked on for over six months. Knowing how much my family was looking forward to the evening resulted in an extra amount of self-imposed pressure to successfully complete the transaction, which did take place. Our evening began with the arrival of a long, black limousine at our front door. We got into the limousine, had a lot of laughs talking and joking about the experience, headed for the finest restaurant in town, and had a marvelous time.

Communications Barrier 3: Not Putting Your Ego Aside

One business owner was very involved in pushing a particular bill through her state legislature that would be quite beneficial for her business. After the bill had passed with an overwhelming majority in the state's house of representatives, she began the process again on the state's senate side. Unfortunately, the senate handler she felt would be most useful in getting the bill passed did not welcome advice or input from women.

Her strategy was for a male lobbyist to present the position to the senator without stating that it was prepared by a woman. The senator agreed with the positions and became the handler. He was able to get the bill passed on the senate side, and the governor signed the bill. In order to gain the greatest chance of making her plan happen, the woman swallowed her pride and decided to use someone other than herself to do the communicating. Can you imagine the CEO of a publicly owned company taking such a backseat position? The business owner got the results she wanted because she did not let her ego get in the way and did not have to concern herself with recognition.

Who is the most effective person to communicate each of your Personal Plans? The initial reaction of most business owners is, "Of course I am." GEMs know that the reality is that they may not be the best ones to communicate in order to get the results they desire. The best person to do the communicating may be a family member, spouse, or employee. GEMs don't let their egos stop them from using the most effective person to do the communicating.

The typical entrepreneurial nature is to cut to the chase and make things happen quickly. However, taking the indirect—and sometimes more time intensive—route of communications is sometimes the most effective way to get what you want.

You may want to bring in a third party to facilitate the communication of a Personal Plan. If so, who should the third party be? In family businesses it is often more effective to have facilitators meet with family members to explain parts of your Personal Plan and facilitate the discussion of it than it is for you to be the communicator. It is not uncommon for a business owner to ask a TAB facilitator-coach to attend a company planning team meeting. The facilitator-coach makes a formal presentation of the owner's desires and facilitates the planning team discussion.

You may even decide it is most effective to split the communications responsibility between two or more people. Sometimes the team approach to a presentation has the potential to be more effective. In many cases a business owner will partner with his or her TAB facilitator-coach to make a presentation. It may be slightly more difficult to create the structure for two or more people to share the oral presentation and answer questions, but the benefits from doing so can be enormous.

Communications Barrier 4: Not Communicating the Knowledge in Your Head

One business owner I know struggled with trying to figure out why his employees were not carrying out his directions properly on a consistent basis. He said he had a picture in his head of exactly what he wanted and that he had given his employees what he felt were explicit instructions, but they still were unable to produce the expected results.

I suggested that he ask his employees why they were not able to carry out his directions. The following month he met with me again and reported that his employees had stated that they felt his communications had been clearly understood by all. He discovered that his employees simply did not have the knowledge to do what he was asking them to do.

One of the communications barriers business owners regularly face is effectively communicating the knowledge that is in their heads to those employees who are crucial to making their Personal Plans happen. The instructions you give to your employees, even if they are crystal clear, may be difficult for employees to fully carry out because they lack the experience and knowledge that you personally have. It is not enough to merely tell someone "to do it." You can't just assume your employees know "how to do it."

GEMs smash though this barrier by asking their employees what information they need so they can do their best job. Employees will not be able to access your knowledge and experience unless you communicate to them that you want to share them. GEMs work hard at communicating the skills they have that are required to make things happen but that others may not possess. They know that the insight into self-knowledge and knowing how to share it is powerful.

One year TAB's planning team decided to offer a session at our Summer International Facilitator Conference that would focus on Strategic Business Leadership, which is TAB's proprietary planning process for business owners. The planning team agreed that the session would deliver not just information about the topic but also provide everything the facilitators would need to obtain talks on the topic and deliver the talks including PowerPoint presentations, accompanying scripts, and marketing materials.

I possess knowledge that I knew could be very helpful in creating what was needed for this session. I asked the planning team members what they required from me so that they could do the best job possible in packaging the session. By asking what I could do to help, I created a safe environment for the planning team members to open up to me. In response, they asked me to provide certain materials on the topic that I had written, and they felt comfortable asking me questions and to review and discuss their work with them. Together we came up with ways that I could help make the session more valuable.

Results-Driven Communications Checklist

Before we move to the next Secret, Negotiating to Make It Happen, let's recap some of the factors in Results-Driven Communications:

- Keep all channels of communication open under all conditions and on all levels. The TABenos exercise is an excellent method of doing this.
- Get as much information about your plans as possible out of Pocket by determining who is critical to making your Personal Plans happen and telling them as much as possible regarding what you are trying to accomplish and why.
- Adjust or adapt your communications techniques to the personality needs of others based on their individual personality traits.
- Choose the location for your communications based on the purpose of the meeting and the person or group of people with whom you need to communicate.
- Determine with what size group you want to communicate.
- Give a clear message of your accountability expectations by using head-on communications.
- Always be in control of your emotions while communicating.
- Create and distribute a written Company Culture Statement, and take action to enforce it.
- A written agenda will keep meetings on target and prevent them from going off on tangents that take away from the primary focus of the meeting.

- Predetermine the timing of your communications, and stick to it.
- Ask yourself if family members of employees should be included in some aspects of your plans to help make them happen.
- Back up your communications in writing.
- Bypass direct reports when needed.
- Communicate your expectations to create self-motivation.
- Determine who will be the best one to communicate your message.
- Communicate the knowledge that is in your head to those employees who are crucial to making your Personal Plans happen.

CHAPTER 5

THE SECRET OF
NEGOTIATING TO MAKE IT HAPPEN

At dinner one night with a group of business owners, a successful Las Vegas business owner stated that her biggest challenge in achieving her Personal Plans was handling the family and business negotiations needed to make her plans happen. As the conversation opened up to include everyone seated at the table, it turned out that the biggest problem for several in the group was their lack of skill in handling negotiations to make their Personal Plans happen.

Not all of your Personal Plans will require negotiating skills to get results, but many of them will. The lack of good negotiating skills is a factor that keeps many business owners from maximizing their success both in their personal and businesses lives. In contrast, GEMs never underestimate the importance of using superior negotiating skills to make their Personal Plans happen.

Most business owners operate under the false assumption that the negotiation process is limited to the deal maker. But GEMs use their negotiating skills to get successful results in situations from which lesser negotiators have walked away because they believed that getting something to happen was impossible.

Negotiating happens so naturally during the day-to-day process of our lives that we often don't even realize we are doing it.

So you may have more experience in negotiating than you think you do. For example, you are often negotiating when you discuss with your spouse or partner who is going to go to the grocery store or who is going to get up the next time the baby cries.

Similarly, in business, you are often negotiating when you purchase equipment, products, or services or when you are resolving issues such as employee pay raises. You typically also need to negotiate to get business financing, buy or lease a new building, outsource manufacturing or services, and develop strategic alliances.

When I was a teenager, my father often allowed me to sit in while business deals were being made. I feel fortunate to have been exposed to different levels of negotiations skills from such an early age. It was clear to me almost from the beginning that successful negotiating requires a certain aptitude that some people naturally have to a greater extent than others.

Over the years I have watched and learned from other negotiators I have been exposed to—both good and bad—and I have incorporated what I learned into the Secret of Negotiating. Regardless of your negotiating aptitude, the Secret of Negotiating will greatly improve your negotiating skills and take them to the level that you need to make it happen.

I do not expect you to mirror my—or anyone else's—negotiating techniques. GEMs don't try to negotiate as if they were someone else. Instead, they choose techniques used successfully by others and adapt them to their own particular personality style. Modify the techniques set forth in this chapter so they fit your own basic personality and the specific needs of each of your Personal Plans.

There are two steps to the Secret of Negotiating. The first step is to prepare for negotiations as described below in the Seven Preparation Guidelines followed by GEMs. The second step is to learn and implement the Ten Negotiating Techniques used by GEMs to be effective and successful during their negotiations.

Step 1: Prepare for Negotiations Using the Preparation Guidelines Followed by GEMs

Preparation Guideline 1: Know as Much as Possible about Your Opponent

Before I met for a negotiation aimed at creating a possible strategic alliance between The Alternative Board and a particular health-care provider, I called and spoke to a few of the health-care provider's competitors as well as another party who was already in an alliance with the provider. I felt that they might be able to enlighten me as to how the health-care provider might act during negotiations. The information they shared gave me an edge before I entered into the negotiation.

GEMs research their opponent's negotiating strengths and style whenever possible. Knowing how the opposition works will give you a direct route to a successful result. The more important the negotiations are, the more crucial it is that you go into the negotiation knowing as much as possible about your opponent. Fortunately, the Web has made doing this research far easier than it once was.

Tim Hickey, a TAB facilitator-coach in Salem, New Hampshire, says, "Information about those with whom you are negotiating is right at your fingertips due to the advances in telecommunications, video communications, and the Internet. It takes a short time to learn about whom you are negotiating with and their needs. Take the time to educate yourself to their needs so you can take a smarter approach to your negotiations. See their big picture and attempt to reach an agreement by attacking the issue from the other side."

Check more than one source of information about your opponents before entering negotiations. This will help you verify that you have your facts correct. Also compile a list of what the other side is likely to want and what their arguments will probably be before you start negotiations. This will allow you to plan your negotiating responses to justify your position. The more information you have about your opponents' needs, the easier it will be to look for ways to get your opponents to mentally unlock from their "must haves" and open up to alternatives that meet your criteria and also satisfy their needs.

I discovered that a manufacturer was operating at substantially less than full capacity while preparing for an upcoming negotiation. I went into the negotiation determined to use this knowledge to get terms that the manufacturer did not typically offer. My prepared materials allowed me to show the manufacturer how the orders I could get would help get the company back to near capacity. This justified the special terms I was requesting and allowed me to get what I needed from the negotiation.

Preparation Guideline 2: Identify Your Needs

I had a plan to refinance a shopping center I owned in three years time. There was an empty space for rent in the shopping center at the time I created the plan. I calculated that I needed the rent for the empty space to average $12 per square foot in order to create the market value I would need to refinance the center.

The CEO of a company that was a potential tenant for the space stated that his company could not justify paying more than $11 per square foot. I offered a solution that was able to satisfy both of us. The solution was to cut down on the rent his company would pay during the first and second years of occupancy to $10 and $11, respectively, per square foot in return for a third-year rent of $12 per square foot. This amount would give me what I would need when I planned to refinance the center. In this case I made concessions for the first two years of the lease but still stayed within the range of the needs that I had identified for the very important third year of the lease.

You will be able to conduct your negotiations with far more confidence when you go in knowing your own strengths, needs, and the results you desire. In defining what you need out of a negotiation, separate what you would like to have from what you must have—your needs from your wants. Create a list of what you feel is absolutely nonnegotiable, and memorize your objectives and your alternative positions. Your goal is to be able to present your information naturally without looking as if you are reading stiffly from an outline. If your needs involve the timing of an event, make a note of the exact dates and then stay firm to this need in your negotiations. If you are looking at a situation that involves a quantitative factor, such as a specific maximum purchase price, write down the specific amount or numbers involved, and make sure you stay firm on those figures.

Many negotiators have failed to achieve what they needed because they entered the negotiations with a vague expectation such as, "I will try to get the best deal I can get." When your needs are clearly and specifically identified prior to entering the negotiation, you will be able to visualize successfully meeting your specific goals. The firm knowledge of the terms you need will also be quite useful in determining which way to go if a surprise change occurs in the course of the negotiations.

Don't put yourself in a position where there is a must-win on each issue or where you are operating without a fallback position. When you look for your needs versus wants, do not limit yourself to the current situation. Consider the possibility of future relationships or orders you may want to have with your negotiating adversary. Know what your longer-range needs are, and be prepared to use this potential benefit to show how a win-win conclusion can be reached.

Preparation Guideline 3: Train for Big Fights

TAB facilitator-coach Barba Hickman knows one CEO of a data management firm in Colorado whose company has a 90 percent success rate in negotiating the contracts they seek to win. The

CEO uses reverse role playing to prepare for negotiating key contracts or conflicts with critical clients. He assigns one of his employees to play his role and to apply his key messages. The CEO takes the role of the challenger or key client. This allows him the opportunity to test-drive his ideas and to evaluate the strengths and weaknesses that exist. It also gives him some insight into his adversary.

The CEO uses the best of what he observes during the reverse role playing in the actual negotiation. Not only does the CEO come away from the practice exercise with broader ideas and greater confidence, but his employees learn how to negotiate and how to treat clients with respect.

How many times have you heard someone say that a winning prizefighter earned more than $1 million for less than an hour's work? Of course that statement is misleading. That hour is only the fighter's "public time" and does not recognize the grueling hours spent in training to prepare for the actual fight. Just like prizefighters, GEMs dedicate themselves to preparing for negotiations by practicing and through role-play interaction. Putting your best prenegotiation preparation together is as important as hard training is for the "million-dollar-an-hour" prizefighter.

You are not going to take the time to do a rehearsal for your small impact day-to-day negotiations. But if the results of the negotiations are important to making your plans happen, take the time to go through a role-playing session rehearsal. The rehearsal should include interactions involving what you expect to happen at the real negotiation using questions you think are likely to be asked of you, as well as your replies. This rehearsal will be more productive if it includes someone in a role-playing capacity who knows how your adversary thinks and acts in negotiations.

The best way to become a better negotiator is to practice. Become more aware of the day-to-day negotiations that you face, and use these experiences to fine-tune your negotiating skills. You have a great deal of negotiating strength in your body movements so practice controlling your body movements before you need to use the skill so that the movements look natural. Properly used, body power will have great impact and become a powerful negotiating tool.

GEMs use their body movements to control people and situations in negotiations. Good eye contact is one very effective body-power tool. Direct eye contact lets you express power without having to raise your voice. Practice looking directly into your opponent's eyes when you are making an important point. The more intense the eye contact, the more intense the message you are sending.

Be honest with yourself and get feedback from others you trust, who have seen you negotiate, about any body movements or facial expressions that you use that become forced and unnatural during negotiations. Forced body movements will tip off experienced opponents that you are uncomfortable and will indicate to them that you have a lack of confidence in your position.

Preparation Guideline 4: Know the Subject of the Negotiations

I have participated in negotiations in which very early on it became apparent that my opposition did not have a high level of understanding of the business area involved in the negotiation. It was easy to use the lack of understanding to my own advantage to help get what I wanted out of the negotiations.

In every business field there are nuances and terminology specific to the field. It is important that you have at least a basic understanding of this terminology or jargon. Your credibility during a negotiation will be undermined if you make a statement about the industry that your opponent recognizes as being inaccurate. You would not, for instance, effect a very powerful argument when negotiating a loan request if you did not understand the financial terminology the lender is likely to use in any questions.

Preparation Guideline 5: Try to Control the Meeting Setting

When the stakes are high, try to conduct your negotiations face-to-face (in person or via videoconferencing) rather than over the telephone, or even worse, via e-mail. Unless you are able to see the other person, or people, with whom you are negotiating, you will not be able to observe the key facial and body language signals that will let you know what they are really feeling and thinking.

Where you meet to negotiate can influence your adversary to give you the attention you need and the enthusiastic backing you want for your proposal. The party that has the greatest leverage will ultimately control the location if he or she takes advantage of this leverage. Try to have meetings involving important negotiations at your office. You will feel more comfortable and more in charge of the situation when you are in your own surroundings. If this is not possible, try to have the meeting at a neutral location such as a restaurant rather than at the office of your adversary.

Preparation Guideline 6: The Winning Attitude

TAB facilitator-coach Barba Hickman told me about one CEO who considers every negotiating opportunity to be just a practice session. This eliminates the stress often associated with negotiating. He pretends to be an expert negotiator who is simply observing the negotiation process. Then, as he is negotiating, he listens to his "internal expert negotiator" and modifies his approach as needed to ensure a successful outcome. He is less interested in winning a specific outcome (dollar figure) than he is in winning the customer for life.

Pick the attitude you want to use to accomplish your negotiating objective before you go into the negotiation. The attitude you choose will differ based on many factors including such things as the leverage you have and how much you need for the negotiations to work. The attitude you take during negotiations will often depend on the personality or behavior of the people with whom you are negotiating. With some people you will have no alternative but to be more "in their face" than with other people.

There will be some people with whom you have to negotiate in business and life whose personalities will clash with yours. Some people you negotiate with will even have a "bulldog" mentality with which they attempt to force ideas down your throat. Not everybody is going to be your friend. This does not mean, however, that you cannot work successfully together. GEMs embrace the attitude that they can successfully negotiate with people they do not like in order to make their Personal Plans happen.

Go into negotiations with confidence, but leave your ego outside the door. Ego and vested interest are a combination that makes it hard for many negotiators to be totally objective. Deep down your attitude has to include the view that negotiating is a game. It is not life and death. This attitude is something that is well understood in many areas of the world such as the Far East and the Middle East. You will not be respected in these countries if you do not counteroffer on a proposal, no matter how attractive the original proposal seems. Unfortunately, in the Western world, too many people look down on the art of negotiating and don't understand that it can be fun.

I generally look forward to my business negotiating activities. This doesn't mean that I have enjoyed every aspect of every business negotiation activity I have been a part of, but I have enjoyed most of the negotiations I have participated in. I have never had to push myself to think about an important upcoming business negotiation. To the contrary, I have had to make an effort to stop thinking about what I will need to prepare for and best handle the negotiations.

Preparation Guideline 7: Breaking the Ice before Negotiating

During a trip overseas I had the opportunity to enter into preliminary negotiations with the owner of an audio equipment manufacturing company. Several people in the industry had warned me that they saw my adversary as a tyrant. I went into the negotiation prepared for someone who would be very difficult to deal with.

Upon entering the man's office for the meeting, I could not help but notice his collection of vintage record players. I commented on how fascinating I found both the equipment and the whole evolution of the recording industry. He smiled warmly at me and asked me if I would like to see the rest of his collection.

He brought me to a separate room that was stacked with vintage players. He started out by telling me the history of some of his favorite pieces. This evolved into small talk about his family and his views on such things as the importance of employees' taking exercise during the workday. This all occurred before we had one word of discussion relating to the business negotiation about which we were scheduled to meet. I am convinced that our eventual negotiation went so well because of the easy rapport we developed over a shared interest.

Most people have a tendency to want to get into the purpose of a negotiation too quickly. This can be especially detrimental if you are meeting with someone for the first time. People like to do business with people they know, like, and trust. While a trusting relationship takes more time to build than you may have available for the negotiation, you should still try to take 5 to 10 minutes at the beginning of the negotiations to break the ice over topics of interest on which you and your adversary can connect. That way, you will at least have a good jump start in building such a relationship.

There are a lot of interesting questions or topics you can bring up that will create a more relaxed and open atmosphere. However, your efforts to break the ice will not be effective if they are insincere or based on a set of contrived questions. Ideally you want to find a neutral commonality shared by both you and your adversary and use this to establish camaraderie. The warm-up is not about sharing deep personal secrets or giving away anything that will give your adversary an edge.

While I prefer to meet for negotiations on my own turf, if I am meeting outside of my own office, my warm-up often springs off of something I observe in my adversary's office or the place where we are meeting. Sports or recreation-related topics are typically an area about which most people feel comfortable talking. Give some thought to the types of things about which you are comfortable talking that may also be of interest to others. Once you feel that the ice has started to melt, ask follow-up questions that can be easily answered and have the potential to warm things up even more.

There are definite subjects that are taboo to the warm-up session. You always take a big chance by bringing up any topic that could be volatile. For instance, you want to avoid discussing politics and religion unless you know exactly where the other person stands on these subjects. Also avoid gossip or saying anything bad about the competition—yours or theirs.

Above all, refrain from sharing any stories that are in questionable taste. I once sat in on a negotiation meeting between two companies. The meeting started with general conversation aimed at the parties getting to know one another before the negotiation began. Things were going extremely well until one of the participants told an inappropriate story about someone whom all at the meeting knew. This changed the whole atmosphere of the meeting and created a barrier between the sides that greatly affected the tone of the negotiation.

Ask about your opponent's personal interests. I once noticed a picture of what appeared to be a family member and a horse on the desk of a man who had asked me to his office to negotiate a deal. I casually asked about his interest in horses. After hearing about his interest in riding, I told him about my horses and how great it was for me to share trail riding with my daughters and grandchildren. This "horse talk" softened him from the stoic first impression he had given me and led to a cooperative relationship in which he later opened up as to what he really needed out of our negotiations.

Allow your opponent the opportunity to identify with you and, if possible, make a connection with you. Let your adversary know about you as a person by casually mentioning some of your hopes, aspirations, and interests. The more your opponent gets to know you and can identify with you, the harder it will be for that person to be unreasonable with you once negotiations start.

Now that you know how to prepare for your negotiations, let's take a look Ten Negotiating Techniques that GEMs use during the actual negotiation.

Step 2: Learn and Implement the Negotiating Techniques Used by GEMs

Negotiating Technique 1: Find the Decision Maker

Goethe is quoted as saying, "The man who occupies the first place seldom plays the principal part." If possible, conduct your negotiations only with the party who makes the final decisions. This isn't always easy to do. The final decision maker may believe that his or her time is too valuable to spend with you until he or she has more facts and so will send a subordinate to feel out the situation. Many subordinates enter negotiations acting as if they have full power to negotiate a deal when, in fact, their power is limited.

If you are not sure, directly ask the person with whom you are negotiating if he or she has the authority to finalize the transaction in all respects. You will generally receive an honest answer, but unless you ask the question, the information may not be volunteered. Often the subordinate has the authority to say no to a deal but can approve the deal only if it meets specific criteria. The problem with this is that you may make all your concessions to the subordinate and have no ammunition left to offer the person with the power.

There will be times when you are effectively blocked from meeting with the person with the final decision power. When you are forced to negotiate with a subordinate, you are relying on your adversary's ability to convince his or her boss to accept your proposal. You are asking your opponent, in effect, to negotiate for you. It is likely that your proposals will be insufficiently communicated to the person who makes the final decision.

If your only option is to proceed by negotiating with someone who is sent by the decision maker, follow the negotiation up by sending comprehensive copies of your proposal along with the justifications and benefits relating to your proposal to the person with final authority. Also send memorandums of your meetings with the subordinate so that the final decision maker can better see the big picture of what you are trying to accomplish.

When you find yourself negotiating against a team of individuals, find out which person on the team, if any, ultimately calls the shots. Probe this matter very directly. You do not want to waste your time trying to sell to the wrong person. Don't rely on titles to indicate who has the decision-making authority. Also do not misread the situation when one of the people on the opposite team is doing all the talking and others are quiet. The quiet ones may be the ones calling the shots. Ask who among the team members has the responsibility to make the final decisions. After you have determined who possesses the final authority, direct your attention to that person.

Occasionally your opponents will have joint authority. I negotiated a real estate deal with two sellers who had equal ownership of the property. At first it seemed that dealing with a joint-authority situation required that I convince two people instead of one. It did not take long for me to identify that one person of those with joint authority was dominant. Once this was determined, I focused on selling what I wanted to only that person. The dominant party can be identified by observing how the two parties interact. Does one lean toward the other as if seeking affirmation? Normally, one will become more assertive, and this is the person to whom you should make your strongest appeal.

Negotiating Technique 2: Bridge the Trust Gap

I once sat in on a labor negotiation wherein a labor representative said, "I don't care how good their offer is, it won't be good enough, and I won't accept it." This sort of mental lock is a response that shows a barrier to trust that is difficult to break through.

GEMs know the importance of establishing trust before trying to influence others to support their plans. Trust is built through a process of bridging the gap that naturally exists between two people. As Jason Zickerman, president of TAB states, "Your chances of succeeding in a negotiation will increase as the basic respect increases between the negotiating parties."

There are many ways to develop a trusting relationship. One way is to give the other people information that is meaningful to them.

During a negotiation to buy a company, I told the current owner that my team had found some serious problems in his company's operation that apparently were unknown to him. A correction of this problem would help the owner if the deal did not go through. Prior to my comments, the owner had approached me with suspicion, but after my comments were found to be true, the negotiating relationship became creative and productive.

You can help bridge the trust gap during negotiations by expressing to your adversaries that you are not trying to take advantage of them and that you want a fair deal. Explain that if you have an understanding of your adversaries' needs, you will try to help them meet those needs within the framework of what you need. Be sensitive to the ego and other emotional needs of your opponent. Some people you deal with in business will make irrational or unrealistic demands. GEMs aim at moving the opposition beyond irrational or unrealistic expectations by trying to get them to look at what they would do if they were in the GEM's shoes. This approach can be the linchpin to negotiating a great deal.

Once the trust gap is bridged, it is much easier to develop potential rational and realistic solutions that lead toward negotiating a good resolution. GEMs attempt to get what they want while sending the other party or parties away feeling secure in the knowledge that no one took advantage of them.

Negotiating Technique 3: Be Impersonal

During his last coaching session before retiring, one business owner told me that he had never liked the owner of the fabricator who for decades had been a major supplier for his company. He said, "We were never friends, but I always did my best to get along with him and never let my negative feelings about him interfere with our negotiations."

Be as impersonal in your negotiating tactics as possible. TAB facilitator-coach Tim Hickey says, "When negotiating, it is important to keep in mind what the goal is to avoid letting emotions get in the way. Stay focused on the issue, and don't let the personalities of those with whom you are negotiating create an obstruction. Keep to the goal at hand, and look at the interests of both parties and what needs to be accomplished. Most importantly, look for ways for both parties to obtain mutual gain."

GEMs resolve negotiations in a way that helps their plans succeed without trying to establish who is right and who is wrong. They focus on the action, not the person. It is important that you make those involved in your negotiations aware of the need to achieve a certain objective and how to do so in as impersonal a manner as possible.

It is not okay to make inflammatory statements or to make an attack statement that puts the person with whom you are negotiating on the defensive. Remember, the people with whom you are negotiating have needs that may be in conflict with yours, but they should not be treated as the enemy. They are playing a role in negotiations just as you are, and you should respect that fact.

Negotiating Technique 4: Ask Questions to Pry Open Undisclosed Information

Early in my career I represented a party who was unwilling to pay more than $750,000 for the purchase of a real estate site. The owner of the property was unwilling to sell for less than $1 million. I reviewed the comparable sales prices of other properties in the area with the owner. I pointed out that the price he was asking for his property was far more than any of the comparable properties. He admitted that his price was too high compared with similar land recently sold in the area. He said he didn't need the money and that he was asking that price in order to have the last laugh on certain relatives who had given him a bad time 15 years earlier when he bought the property for a price that they felt was too high. Psychologically, he wanted to be able to tell them he had sold the property for $1 million.

I satisfied his emotional need by agreeing to a contract for $1 million that involved a $100,000 payment to him on the date of purchase with the remainder of the amount spread over 10 years with no interest payments. The key to the deal was the lack of interest payments. This resulted in the true cost of the purchase price being less than the total payments for a purchase price of $750,000 with $650,000 of it paid out over 10 years at the interest rates typical of the time. The seller was able to brag that he had received $1 million for the land, and the buyer got the property he wanted for the price he wanted. Both parties satisfied their needs, and it was truly a win-win situation.

Ask questions at the negotiation session that will uncover helpful information. Often your questions will pry out information that your opponent is not hiding but has simply not thought about. The information you uncover may be a deal changer or breaker.

When negotiating to buy a company, I always ask questions of the current owner such as, "Do you have any new competition coming into the picture?" and "Do you have any personnel pressure?" One business owner responded casually to my questions that several of the service technicians had recently talked about unionizing. The potential changes to the cost of operating and even potential shutdown of the stores because of the possibility that the employees would unionize told me that I should back off from buying the business because it was too risky.

Once when negotiating the purchase of a real estate property, I asked the seller if he had any tax needs that could be helped by the structure of the deal. The question resulted in information about what he wanted but did not think could be helped by the deal structure. I contacted a top-level tax attorney who suggested a structure for the transaction that neither of the negotiating parties had even considered. The structure satisfied the seller's needs and was also a great deal for me.

Negotiating Technique 5: Project an Image of Having Leverage

During the Vietnam War the United States had nuclear arms capabilities. This apparently did not result in a leverage advantage in negotiating power because all parties involved knew, or thought they knew, that the United States would not use this power. Similarly, if you are negotiating with someone and that person knows that you will not follow through on a threat, the threat has no negotiating power. You have no leverage unless the opposition believes that you intend to act on what you say you are going to do.

Negotiations are often based on leverage or the perception of leverage. Consider the number of times billion-dollar companies have been brought to their knees by unions that have only a fraction of the companies' financial resources. The unions had leverage that they turned into negotiating power because groups of workers were willing to follow persuasive union leaders to bring negative impact on the companies.

Sometimes the perception of power is more important than actual power. However, potential power will not change decisions at the bargaining table if the opposition believes it will not be used. Potential power does not mean anything in the negotiating process if it cannot realistically be put into action.

Negotiating Technique 6: Watch for and React to Nonverbal Clues

TAB facilitator-coach Barba Hickman offers the following simple suggestions for how to watch for and react to the nonverbal communication clues of the people with whom you are negotiating. Hickman says that when your opponents cross their arms or shake their heads, you should change your approach to one that is more friendly or personable. Get your opponents to start talking about some of their interests until the pressure lessens. Try to position your terms in relation to their interests, benefits, or desires. Keep listening and reacting to their nonverbal clues. The best way to persuade others is with your ears, eyes, and a keen sense of personal connection.

GEMs know how to read other people's body language, and they are constantly on the lookout for the nonverbal, physical cues that can help them to direct negotiations where they want them to go. Nonverbal messages are often more likely to communicate the truth than verbal ones. Without this understanding, you are negotiating with one arm tied behind your back.

Examples of nonverbal body signals are almost endless. If the arms of the person with whom you are negotiating are crossed, it may indicate that he or she is not completely comfortable with you or what you are saying. Crossed arms are a sign of protection. If you see a person shrug his or her shoulders while you are talking, it probably indicates that he or she is indifferent to what you are saying or how you are trying to say it.

GEMs are masters at analyzing and interpreting their opponent's subtle facial expressions. GEMs know that facial movement and expression provide nonverbal clues to the true emotions of those with whom they are negotiating. Facial expressions can show surprise, anger, contempt, disgust, fear, happiness, and sadness. The eyebrows, nose, and mouth of your opponent are key areas where cues of these emotions appear.

While some negotiators can quickly disguise their facial expressions, it is difficult for most people to completely stop the automatic response of their facial muscles to their underlying emotions. If you are paying attention, you will not miss the ultra-quick facial movements that signal underlying emotion by even the most talented "actors."

The eyes of your adversary will give clues to their inner thoughts if you are observant. Are they squinting at you in disbelief? Does the positioning of their eyebrows indicate surprise or skepticism of what you are saying? Are they looking you straight in the eye with apparent conviction, or are they avoiding eye contact altogether perhaps because of lack of confidence?

I have negotiated with people who have avoided looking into my eyes while they were presenting what were supposedly their ultimatums. By refusing eye contact, they inadvertently let me know that they were weak in their convictions and were not confident in their ability to convince me.

I recall one woman who pursed her lips before responding no to a needed term for a potential strategic alliance. Without registering any emotion on my part, I reworded the question and asked her again. This time she responded without hesitation that she would go along with terms that excluded a relatively minor factor that was in the original terms I had proposed. If I had not been observing her facial expressions, I might not have caught on that this woman did not have her heart set on turning down the alliance.

Once I made a wrong decision in "reading" someone the first time I negotiated with him because I did not understand the real meaning behind his wide smile. Although certain smiles indicate happiness, I learned that his smile, which appeared to be plastered on his face, showed underlying tension. After I recognized this fact, I looked for it in future negotiations with the man.

I once had to negotiate with an employee who would clam up when he was upset. You could tell he was upset because of the way his nostrils flared. Calm words can be belied by flared nostrils or other facial signals that indicate hidden anger or distress. Tightness around the mouth may signify that there is a lot more tension than your opponent's easygoing manner and casual words may indicate. A frown is likely to indicate dissatisfaction or anger. Many people show they are confused by a tightening in their foreheads or the way that they rub or tug at their ears or noses. Some show they are confused or nervous by biting their lips.

Early in my career I negotiated several times against an attorney who unintentionally tipped me off as to when he was ready to accept an offer by tapping his fingers impatiently on the table or by tapping his right foot. It was a sure sign that he liked what he had heard and wanted to nail down the agreement quickly.

Blushing is an involuntary reaction that some people have when they are embarrassed or lying. I know one general counsel of a company who breaks out in hives if confronted after saying something that is not true or claiming that he has a firm position on something when he really does not.

If a person's seated posture during negotiations is erect at the start but becomes stooped or slouched as the negotiations proceed, it probably means one of two things. It can mean that they believe that they have already lost the argument or it can mean that their energy level is getting low. Either way this leaves them vulnerable to your insistence with a point that you want to make.

Negotiating Technique 7: Reacting Flexibly to the Intimidator

Probably the most unusual negotiation I ever had was with a very successful business owner who yelled throughout our entire negotiations. I realized that it was just his style to yell when he negotiated, and I accepted his style because the deal was important to me. I didn't try "smoothing over" his anger or try to tell him to calm down. Telling someone to calm down may cause a temporary lull, but generally it won't help solve the underlying problem.

At times during the negotiation I laughed at him when he got too off the wall with his speech volume. At other times I let him know that I understood his version of the facts and what he wanted. I verbally played his story back to him using a calm tone of voice. I asked open-ended questions such as "Why do you say that?" and "Tell me more." in order to bring all possible information out in the open. Next I asked specific questions to clarify the situation and bring his objective more clearly into focus. Finally, I verified that I understood his arguments by restating them objectively. I got his confirmation that I understood the situation as he saw it. Once the yeller felt that he had been heard and understood, he saw that the only issue remaining was how to solve the problem.

This story has a follow-up that I certainly did not expect. Weeks later, after we had finalized our deal, the yeller actually commented to me how much he had enjoyed negotiating with me. He then asked if I would be interested in partnering with him on future deals.

You will undoubtedly be forced to negotiate with someone who tries to intimidate you at some time or another. One technique I use to respond to attempts at intimidation or threat tactics during negotiations is looking at the person trying to intimidate me and smiling or laughing. Over the years, this technique has often caused my opponents to realize that their approach is not going to work with me.

I sat in one negotiation where one party, who is around 6 feet 3 inches tall, moved within inches from being nose to nose with a business owner with whom he was negotiating who is around 5 feet 6 inches tall. The taller man did this with the objective of putting himself in the power position. The shorter business owner smiled and simply said, "Jim, you are invading my space. If you want to get anywhere with our discussion, you will have to back off."

GEMs don't "freak out" over negotiating challenges or when their opponent tries to intimidate them. In fact, GEMs are more likely to get psyched up with the challenge of winning the negotiations. It is a matter of attitude. Be prepared to win against the negotiator who tries to intimidate you.

Experienced negotiators have used intimidation tactics to break down many bright but less inexperienced opponents who succumb to embarrassment or fear and wind up accepting terms they would not have previously considered. At a time when I was a young attorney representing my employer, the May Department Stores, I had to negotiate a strategic alliance with a company represented by an adversary who had several decades of experience negotiating such agreements. Although I had very little negotiating experience, I was well prepared, and I made an honest presentation of why my terms were fair.

My adversary waited until the end of my presentation, looked at the other members of his team, and said, "Based on Fishman's comments, he clearly has not been around long enough to know all the hurdles to be faced before this project can be a success." His comments were intended to intimidate me but instead they infuriated me. My response was not to come back with my own sarcastic comments, although I was tempted to do so. I calmly turned, looked him in the eye, and stared him down with an expression that my mom has always referred to as my "evil-eye look." My reaction surprised him. You could see the change in his confidence level when no one at the table said a word. My intent was to let him know that I understood the insult and was not going to let it interfere with my reaching my objectives.

After several seconds of staring, I calmly stated that if their company was not interested in being part of the strategic alliance under the terms my company envisioned, I would be delighted to call one of their competitors—mentioning two of them by name to show that I knew their company was not the only game in town.

Negotiating Technique 8: Appeal to Hearts and Minds

It is a mistake to look at negotiations from a one-sided view that is centered on only your desire. The objective in negotiating is to influence another person's decisions through a process that results in coming to an agreement that is compatible with what you need to make your Personal Plans happen. This does not mean that you have to win at the expense of the other party.

When both possible and practical, GEMs take the needed steps to change the issues and interests of a negotiation to a scenario in which both parties satisfy enough of their emotional needs so that they both feel like winners in the outcome. Persuading your adversaries that your objectives also satisfy their needs is a technique for successful negotiations. This power to persuade by appealing to the hearts and minds of your adversary is often what moves parties to agreement.

One GEM's philosophy is simple: "To become a successful negotiator, work on encouraging others to think, feel, and act in the way you want. You should appeal not only to their minds but to their hearts as well. Concentrate on addressing their main objectives and, if possible, appealing to their emotions."

Showing how your ideas will benefit your adversary is paramount to successful negotiations. Work to find a benefit that may not have been previously on the bargaining table, ideally something close to the heart of your opponent. This expands the size of the value-benefit pie that is under discussion.

Negotiating Technique 9: Be Patient and Persistent

A business owner with decades of successful negotiating experience once told me that the winner in a negotiation is usually determined by which side has the most "butt power." At first I laughed at his comment not realizing how accurate he was. But after devoting many hours of my life to negotiations, it has become clear to me that many negotiations are won simply because the losing side wasn't persistent enough and was worn down by the other negotiator.

Most people who want their plans to happen have a tendency to be impatient. In contrast, GEMs are patient and persistent in their negotiations. Too many people approach negotiations believing the deal has to get done quickly. This makes them vulnerable because the longer the negotiation process continues, the more they press to come up with an agreement. Ironically, deals that are made too quickly are usually made because one of the parties has left too much on the table and has not done enough counteroffering.

A friend of mine who is an internationally successful businessman says that some of his best deals are the ones he did not make. There may come a time when you can't make it happen with the terms you want and it is better to walk away than to agree to unsatisfactory terms. Too many business owners have experienced negotiating a major deal with terms that did not meet their needs but to which they agreed because they were pressured by their own sense of urgency. This situation can easily occur if you get too emotionally involved.

Pressure in negotiations often arises from time constraints. Your opponents may try to pressure you into making a hasty deal by giving you a deadline whereby you either agree to their terms or their offer is retracted. If this happens to you, do not assume that the deadline given to you is a real deadline. Ask yourself whether there is any logical reason for the deadline to exist. Many of the best deals I have made have taken place long after the deadlines given to me had expired. It just required patience and persistence.

"No" quite often is not the final answer in negotiations. In fact, persistence can turn a "no" into a "yes." Being persistent and repeating the substance of my position has often resulted in changing the views of my opponent. "No" is often an indicator that you just need to change your strategy and attack the negotiations differently.

Negotiating Technique 10: End the Meeting at the Right Moment

I once offered a specific amount of money that I said was my final offer for the acquisition of a company I wanted. The owner came back with a slightly higher figure. I let the deal die because it was more important in this situation that I maintained my reputation for letting a deal die if my final offer was not met than it was to acquire the company. If I had not held firm, the broker representing the company I wanted would have known that my final offers were not really my final offers. He also possibly could have conveyed this information to other mergers-and-acquisitions brokers. This would have hurt future deals I had planned to make.

Make a conscious effort to pick the right time to end a negotiations meeting. This time may or may not be before you come to a resolution. There are three signs to look for in determining when to stop before reaching a resolution.

The first sign is when emotions start getting out of control. This situation has the effect of closing minds to logical ways of resolving a conflict. The second sign is when you find the conversation becoming circular because some or all of the participants are feeling defensive. In these situations, it is best to call the meeting to a halt and determine a date to resume the discussion. Ask the participants to think of new ways to resolve the problem before the next meeting. The third sign is when continuing the meeting will destroy your credibility that a "final offer" really is a final offer.

GEMs know that the reputation they develop from previous negotiations strongly affects their bargaining power for the future. If you cave in on items you say are must-haves today, it can hurt you the next time you negotiate with the same party or others who find out what you have done.

When you do decide it is a waste of everyone's time to continue negotiating, summarize your proposal and value points. Then announce that at this point there will be a break in the negotiations.

Negotiating Checklist

Before we move on to the next Secret, Creativity to Make It Happen, let's recap some of the factors in Negotiating to Make It Happen:

- Resolve negotiations by trying to create a win-win situation.
- Don't try to establish who is right and who is wrong.
- Enter negotiations knowing as much as possible about the strengths, needs, and desired results of your opponent.
- Enter negotiations knowing exactly what you need out of the negotiation.
- Rehearse before you enter the negotiation, and consider answers to questions you think are likely to be asked of you.
- Use body power to control people and situations.
- Have a base understanding of the terminology or jargon essential to your negotiation.
- Try to have meetings involving important negotiations at your own office.

- Pick the attitude you want to use to accomplish your negotiating objective.
- Break the ice at the start of negotiations over topics of interest on which you and your adversary can connect.
- Find the decision maker.
- Establish trust before trying to influence others.
- Remain impersonal, and don't let your emotions get in the way.
- Ask questions to pry open undisclosed information.
- You have no real leverage unless you intend to act on what you say you are going to do.
- Understand how to read the body language of others.
- Be prepared for the negotiator who tries to intimidate you.
- Appeal to your opponent's heart and mind.
- Be patient and persistent.
- Know when to end the negotiation.

CHAPTER 6

THE SECRET OF
CREATIVITY TO MAKE IT HAPPEN

You will have some Personal Plans that are so basic in nature that a great deal of creativity will not be required to make them happen. However, the development and execution of many of your Personal Plans will test your creative ability to its limits. By learning how to set your imagination free, you will be opening the door to a tremendous power that can bring successful new ideas and solutions.

Most business owners fail to access their full creativity because they allow time obstructions to creativity to get in their way or because they simply do not know how to access their creative abilities. In contrast, GEMs are continually on the lookout for creative ideas that will move their companies and lives to the next level. Creative ideas can range from the astonishing and brilliant to the simply practical. GEMs maximize their creativity by pushing aside the unnecessary time obstructions that block their creative abilities. They continually flex their creative muscles and keep their creative juices flowing.

The Secret of Creativity is composed of two elements. The first element is good time management that allows you the time you need to give to applying your energy and attention to the creative process. If you can't free yourself from your day-to-day problems and other obstacles, you won't have the time to be creative. Most business owners are functioning on overload; working more hours than they want and never getting ahead, or getting ahead much too slowly. You can tap into your true creative resources only when you are removed from the day-to-day distractions and unnecessary commitments that keep you from focusing on what is truly important to creating the success and happiness you desire.

The second element in the Secret of Creativity is applying creativity-producing techniques to boost your creative abilities in order to make your Personal Plans happen. If you are not creative in your approaches to solving problems and opening the door to new ideas and opportunities, the results won't happen.

Let's take a look at the first element, Time Management.

Time Management

To successfully embark on the creative thought process, you must first create the time in which to freely unleash the inventive genius inside you. Working under the gun of time pressure counteracts most peoples' creative abilities. Even the most successful GEMs are hard-pressed to come up with their best creative ideas, solutions, and methods for making it happen when they are working under time pressures.

Poorly managing your time and allowing distractions and obstacles to eat away at your time will prevent you from ever being able to fully engage with the problem or situation you are facing to make your Personal Plans happen. Most business owners are so busy putting out the day-to-day fires at work that they remain stuck in the rut of doing things the way they have always been done—for better or worse. They never find the time to discover new solutions and opportunities that will allow them to rise to the next level of success, and they rarely reach the pinnacle of their dreams.

In contrast, GEMs create open time periods that are devoid of obstacles in which to maximize their creative potential. The Alternative Board acquaints members with the following Seven Time Management Obstacles that are common to most business owners and teaches them how to overcome these obstacles that block their time and thwart them from accessing their full creative forces.

Time Management Obstacle 1: Not Tackling Tasks That Need to Be Done because They Are Overwhelming in Size or Complexity

One businesswoman I coached told me that she did not have the time to complete her Opportunities Statement because she was just too busy during the workday. I asked her to honestly recount how she had spent the previous night. She rather sheepishly admitted she had spent over two hours playing computer games while important work sat on her desk unfinished. She said she just could not face the commitment of the work she had to do and had used the computer games as an escape.

This businesswoman's situation is anything but unique. Many people become so overwhelmed by the multitude of things that they have to do each day that they avoid doing anything at all. They fill their day with diversions, and their time flies by with no results. In contrast, GEMs do not allow themselves to become intimidated or overwhelmed by the size and complexity of the tasks in front of them. They bring tasks down to size by breaking them into small, manageable pieces, and they make a commitment to finishing what is in front of them.

You will be far less likely to freeze into inaction if you look at a major task from the perspective of how and when you must accomplish each phase of the process. If it is a task that involves multiple steps, create a detailed schedule that lists all the steps involved. Indicate start and completion dates for each step of the

task, and separate out the things that don't have to be done immediately so each day you are looking at only the part of the task
that you absolutely have to address. This will keep you from
becoming overwhelmed by the magnitude of the task at hand.
You will be amazed upon completing steps A, B, and C of a task,
how D and E suddenly become easy.

This technique applies beyond the business spectrum. When
my wife and I were building a house, my wife commented to me
that she felt overwhelmed by the task of making so many choices
about lighting fixtures, carpet, granite, cabinets, and so on. We
sat down and broke down the process into smaller steps. We pri-
oritized the decision-making needs according to what had to be
decided by what date. Breaking the process down and taking the
time to prioritize what decisions needed to be made allowed my
wife to make the needed decisions without feeling overwhelmed
by the large number of decisions she was facing.

One woman, Lakisha, found herself overwhelmed by too many
things to do and too little time in which to do them. She turned
to her TAB Board for help. She admitted she was not getting things
done in a timely fashion and blamed the situation on a list of things
that must be done that contained over 100 items. She claimed there
was no way she could ever catch up let alone get ahead.

I asked her to bring her list to our next coaching session. With
just a quick glance at the list, I easily identified a number of items
that were not only low priority but that probably did not even
have to be done in the next 12 months. I asked Lakisha to put a
check mark next to all the items that absolutely had to get done
the following day. After going through several pages and identifying stray items, it turned out there were only five things that
required her immediate focus.

We continued to break Lakisha's large list down to smaller,
day-to-day lists based on priority status. In the process we completely eliminated 25 items that had either already been done or
no longer needed to be done. We took some items and reduced

the magnitude of them by determining what tasks could be delegated to others. In the end we brought Lakisha's large list down to a total of 50 items that were spread out on a day-to-day basis. Not one of the days had more than five items that needed to be done. Lakisha no longer felt threatened by the things that had to be done, and her anxiety was completely eliminated.

If you start the day without setting up a schedule or a list of priorities for that day, you will likely come up short and find the day stressful because of feeling overwhelmed. Every business owner faces multiple tasks during the business day. It is just the way it is. GEMs identify and prioritize the tasks, activities, and decisions that they need to do each day. The key is to get out of your sight the things that don't have to be done that day.

In determining your priorities for what tasks need to be done each day, ask yourself what will bring about the greatest results. Your answer to this question will clarify the importance of different tasks. There will usually be items on a given day that carry equal importance. When this is the case, find the most undesirable task and accomplish it first. This will relieve much of the dread and allow you to look forward to the rest of the day.

One of the most efficient ways to schedule your time involves creating a things-to-do list. This list works best when it is sorted into three categories. The first category should show recurring weekly items such as meetings with key management members. The second category should deal with items that need to be completed within the next 30 days. Make sure to identify the specific day and time each item should be worked on during the 30-day time span. The third category should identify all low-priority items. These are items that do not have to be completed within 30 days and may not even have a completion date at all. They are just things that have to get done whenever you find an available moment to act on them.

Update the second and third categories of your things-to-do list at the end of each day using realistic timelines. This small investment of your time will give you a big return of available time in which to conjure the creativity needed for making it happen.

Time Management Obstacle 2: Not Learning from Others' Experiences

GEMs don't waste time reinventing the wheel. Learning what others in similar experiences have done that both worked and did not work is a valuable tool that will save you immeasurable time. At TAB Board meetings, members avoid reinventing the wheel by listening to the past experiences shared by other board members. The advice received from fellow board members on how they have attempted similar endeavors in the past and the reasons why they failed provides fellow members with great insight. Given this advantage, members are able to modify their proposed actions so that what created failure for one TAB member is not repeated by another.

Expose yourself to the successes and failures of others by reading books and articles about people who have overcome mistakes to find great success. Don't limit yourself to only business stories; there is much to be learned from looking at both the successes and failures from all areas of life.

Obviously you can't spend the rest of your life just studying what others have done. But the information gleaned from even an hour of studying what others have done will save you many times that hour in return. If, for instance, you are making a decision about whether your company should produce a new product, you would first find out everything you can, within reason, relating to the businesses involved in that product area. Using what you learn from the Web and reading and talking to people who are involved in that product industry will save you time in the long run as it will prevent a lot of avoidable mistakes from being made. It will also inspire you to take what has already been done to greater heights and levels of creativity.

GEMs also take into consideration any past situations that may be analogous to a current challenge. The longer you are in the business world, the easier it is to make a judgment based upon how you responded to certain situations. Learn from your own experiences as well as from the experiences of others.

Time Management Obstacle 3: Not Saying No

Russ could not say no to taking over committee assignments ranging from requests from his trade association to chair a committee to volunteer requests from his religious congregation to family requests. His failure to say no was a major factor behind his inability to make time to get away from day-to-day problems at work. Because he needed what free time he had to manage, he had no time left for creativity.

Too many business owners hurt themselves and keep their companies from getting the benefit of their abilities because they are unwilling to say no. They fall into the trap of saying yes when they really want to say no because they dread the possible confrontation saying no can inspire. They end up doing things they don't want to do and have no time to do, and they often harbor resentment, which steals even more time from the mental space they need to nurture their creativity.

Saying no is a skill you must learn. It takes practice, especially if you are not used to saying it. Don't get caught up in further time loss by offering long explanations of why you have to say no. Absolve yourself from any guilt you may feel in taking back the control of your own life.

Those around you, including family and employees, may react negatively when you use a word they are not used to hearing from you. You may even receive resistance from those who have difficulty accepting change and who may see your use of the word no as a threat to that with which they are familiar. Yes, you may lose some friends who have always been able to get you to do what they want. But are these really people whom you want in your life? Living an authentic life that addresses your needs and dreams does provide challenges, and sometimes there will be unwelcome consequences. But chances are that these consequences will turn out to be blessings in the long run.

Time Management Obstacle 4: Not Getting away from the Telephone

One entrepreneur was involved in several civic and charitable activities in addition to her business. Due to these outside involvements, both her office phone and cell phone were constantly plagued with incoming and outgoing phone calls that were not strictly business calls but that she deemed important. When employees were in her office to discuss work matters, there would always be interruptions for phone calls. During a coaching session, she discussed with me the lack of time she had for creatively addressing her Personal Plans and making them happen. She blamed this on the fact that she could not get away from the telephone long enough to make the needed time.

My recommendation was for the woman to meet with her secretary and ask for help in developing a telephone call screening policy. The business owner reflected on the actual time she spent on unnecessary calls that were preventing her from creating open time for creative development and opportunities. The realization helped her keep the discipline of the new telephone call screening policy.

One of the most common examples of poor time management is partaking in nonemergency, nonbusiness phone calls during working hours. While this practice may seem to be an obvious error in self-management, there are hidden aspects of it that cause complications for many people.

It is important to know how to get people off the phone. I remember one telephone conversation I had with a man who repeated the same thing for over 30 minutes. When I indicated that I had a conference call coming in and needed to get off the phone, he stated that he was offended that I did not have more time for him. He mentioned that he was never rushed off the phone by a particular person who was an executive of the company at that time. That comment helped explain why that particular department head could never finish what he had to do in a timely manner. He obviously was wasting too much time on the phone.

There is an abundance of technology that can provide relief for this problem. Research the system that best suits your needs and financial situation.

Time Management Obstacle 5: Not Establishing Uninterrupted Time for Contemplation

When I started at Tipton, I had an open-door policy. Any employee was welcome to knock on my door and would be invited in to talk to me at any time. My open-door policy was popular and very valuable. Later, as Tipton grew, this policy became a weakness. The interruptions began to increasingly interfere with my ability to focus on my Personal Plans and the creative thinking needed in making them happen.

I didn't give up the open-door policy entirely, but I did have to create a policy that restricted it to designated time periods. It is important to be available to your employees, but you cannot let this distract you from focusing on reaching your dreams.

To enact the modifications to my open-door policy, I sent a memo to my employees. I explained that I wanted employees to feel free to walk into my office—during scheduled blocks of time—to talk, schmooze, or bring up company opportunities and problems. By scheduling specific time blocks, I communicated to my employees that I was open and available to them but also gave myself the benefit of structured time to focus on important matters without employee interruption.

The same time that I blocked for my open-door periods was the scheduled time for me to address small picture matters like signing checks and working on day-to-day problems. If someone came in to speak to me when I was signing checks, I could be interrupted and still return to the task without any difficulty.

Time Management Obstacle 6: Not Delegating

When you take on too many tasks, you can easily become distracted from the focus you need in coming up with creative ideas and Strategies for your Personal Plans. When there is too much on your plate, there will inevitably be problems that arise from the overwhelming number of matters that demand your immediate attention. This is how the "fires" start. So determine if someone else who works for you is qualified to put out the fire. Ask if the fire really justifies keeping you from the time you need to focus on what is really important.

Learning to delegate responsibility when you have too much on your plate will help you avoid this trap. GEMs discipline themselves against taking on more tasks than they can handle. They delegate to others whenever they can, especially in those areas that do not make use of their Competitive Edge Strengths. When you don't delegate, you will inevitably drop the ball on making your Personal Plans happen. Whenever someone can do the job well enough—even if not as well as you can do it—enlist that person's help to get it done.

Time Management Obstacle 7: Not Concentrating on the Future

The owner of one retail shoe store knew his merchandise like few others. However, when I first met him, I judged that he would never grow his business beyond what he was doing in the one store because he constantly, actually obsessively, dwelled on things he had done wrong from the time he was a child. I was not surprised when I met him 10 years later and learned that his business was at the same size that it was when I had first met him. He spent so much time wasting his energy dwelling on things in the past that he could not undo that he did not have the time to come up with creative solutions and opportunities to reach the next level of success.

Have you ever noticed how unsuccessful or even moderately successful people waste time dwelling on what they have done wrong in the past rather than concentrating on the future? You have only so much time and energy. Every minute that you waste obsessing about what you could have done differently under the woulda-coulda-shoulda mindset is time taken from making things happen today.

Now that you understand how to open up the needed time for creative thinking, the next step is learning how to apply the creative techniques that will open your mind to new ideas and ways of doing things that will make your Personal Plans happen.

Development of Your Creative Abilities

For many GEMs, tapping into their creative ability is second nature, but most business owners are heavily challenged when it comes to conjuring their creativity. The creative ideas that GEMs put into place may be variations on what has always been done, or the ideas may be based on new models, technologies, or methods of operating. In some cases the seeds for creative ideas come from outside sources such as advisors or perhaps something the GEM has read or seen.

Children naturally possess the questioning nature that is essential for the development of creativity. Unprompted, children use their imagination and creativity to make play more fun. A child pushing a truck along a floor can mentally transform that floor into a bumpy terrain or a vast superhighway. Ask a young child with a doll or stuffed animal to tell you about his or her plaything and you'll most likely hear a very detailed story. What happens to this creative ability as we grow into adults?

Unfortunately, the response of many parents, teachers, and other adults in response to constant questions children ask is, "Stop asking so many questions." Many children are also told that they should simply accept "what is" without questioning "why." Over time, these kinds of responses, especially from people who are respected in a child's eyes, subconsciously work to undo the natural desire to question.

As adults we still have creative ability, but for many it gets blocked in childhood. Others buy into the belief that they have to think like "adults" which automatically blocks the development of any wild or creative ideas. Many business owners and managers who do not trust their creative instincts formed this pattern because they were never told to trust their instincts while they were growing or were told, "You can't do this. You can't do that."

There are always those who will resist trying to develop their creative skills. Some people adhere to a belief that they are left-brain oriented and that left-brain people are analytical, while right-brain people have all the creativity. This side-of-the-brain argument is just one of many excuses that people use to avoid making the needed efforts to develop their creative abilities. Research shows that creativity is essentially a learned behavior. So even if you cling to the concept of being a left-brain person, rest assured, you still have enough mental talent to develop your creative skills. In other words, everyone is capable of being creative.

Creativity requires a skill that comes more naturally to some people than others. The Alternative Board trains business owners to achieve the success of GEMs by helping them to develop these skills. The good news is that regardless of your natural creativity skill level, barriers to creativity can be broken and your creative skills can be improved. TAB teaches its members that creativity is a skill you can recapture and develop by using the following eight simple and easy-to-use techniques that act as creativity boosters.

> **The same GEM methodology of using creative thinking in the face of challenges to grow your business can also be used when facing challenges in your nonbusiness life.**

Creativity Booster 1: Identify the Real Problem

During a period of time when I was concerned because TAB was not achieving the Goals results in my Plans, I asked one of my top executives what he felt was the reason for this. He replied that too many of our franchisees were diverting their time from increasing TAB memberships because they were taking on unsolicited coaching and consulting projects outside the monthly coaching sessions they were doing for their TAB members.

I spoke to several of the franchisees to get their feedback on what my executive had labeled as the problem. By listening to their views, I zeroed in on the "real" problem, which was quite different from what my executive had identified. I discovered that the basic model for our TAB franchising opportunity was flawed. Armed with the knowledge of the real problem, I created a new franchise opportunity model that became a major factor in bringing TAB to a greater level of success. If I had accepted and tackled my executive's view of the problem, TAB would probably not have become the world's largest franchise system providing peer advisory board and coaching services to business owners.

The first step in creatively solving a problem is to identify the real problem you, or your company, are facing. This involves objectively identifying the real challenge versus what may appear to be the challenge. Gaining this objective view is not always easy, but the bottom line remains that you can't solve a problem if you are addressing the wrong problem.

Business owners, just like nonbusiness owners, often incorrectly view the realities of the actual problem that needs to be solved. Many can't see the situation clearly because they color it with their own emotional baggage or fears, or they simply don't take the time to evaluate all the possibilities. Don't underestimate the time it takes to identify a problem. The process is like taking a trip. The straight line may be the shortest route, but it is not always the best way to go. A longer, more scenic route may provide a look at the unexpected or previously unknown.

It may be a struggle to position yourself so you can objectively see the real problem, but it is crucial that you do so. The clearer you can define the reason why you are in need of an idea, and the potential benefit you desire from that idea, the better you will be able to focus on the narrow area that will lead you to solving the real problem.

Creativity Booster 2: Do Your Homework

When I started doing research for the problem with TAB's franchise opportunity model, I obtained a summary of what the five most successful franchisors that franchised professional business service opportunities were offering to franchise brokers. While conducting this research, I discovered that The Alternative Board was offering less compensation to franchise brokers than were other franchisors. The lower compensation gave brokers less incentive to educate franchise prospects on the TAB opportunity. This knowledge prompted me to create a plan that included paying more competitive commissions to franchise brokers. In turn, this increased TAB's pool of quality franchise prospects.

Do your homework and learn what others are doing to achieve success. Read about and talk to those who are involved in situations similar to yours. As you garner more and more knowledge about a situation, your mind will naturally start to connect the different areas and creative ideas will materialize. You will discard some of these creative ideas once you have analyzed them, but you'll find that enough of them will turn out to be great ideas to justify the time for doing your homework.

Some of your most successful ideas will come from learning what others have already done, and by focusing on how their approach might be fitted to your own circumstances. Pick the brains of people who have experience in the same field as you, but also solicit the help of those in unrelated fields. Someone in a totally different business from yours, who is not hooked into the conventional views of your business, may surprise you with good advice. TAB facilitator-coach Ray Brun says that a TAB Board, due to the diverse backgrounds of its members, all of whom come from noncompeting fields, provides a wealth of genius similar to what the Medicis brought about in the Renaissance era by bringing together artists from all directions.

Creativity Booster 3: Get Away from Thinking about the Problem

Years ago, while we were waiting for our flight at the St. Louis airport, my wife started a crossword puzzle. She began in her usual way by identifying the easy words and then moving on to the more difficult ones. When she reached a point where she was stumped, she put the puzzle away and got out some reading. Later, when we landed in Denver and were waiting for our connecting flight to Aspen, she again got out the puzzle. She was able to identify all the words that had eluded her just hours earlier.

How was my wife able to get around the brick wall that existed in St. Louis? She knew that you shouldn't force a solution to a difficult problem unless it is needed immediately. At times you may find yourself at a standstill for coming up with creative ideas. Your creative juices are more likely to be summoned if you allow your mind to relax and not think about the problem for a while.

Often when I am having trouble summoning my creativity, I put the work aside and focus on another project. Most times I will get ideas even though I am not thinking about the problem, or just as my wife did with her crossword puzzle, I return to the problem at a later time with a renewed freshness that allows me to find the solution. By taking a break, I have not given up; I have simply allowed my subconscious mind the time it needs to work. This method works. Try it.

One very effective way to temporarily get away from the problem is to change your environment. Often this is as simple as getting away from the office. When I started The Alternative Board, my Personal Vision Statement included taking off substantial Free-Thought Time. Free-Thought Time is time when I choose to be free from contact with the office unless it is an emergency. The Free-Thought Time I took away from the company actually moved TAB forward. Most of my creative ideas for TAB have come to me while doing recreational things like biking, horseback riding, hiking, or skiing and not while purposely thinking about TAB.

Don't let guilt force you into the office during Free-Thought Days. As a business owner, you should not worry about structuring your time like that of your employees. The truth is that killing yourself working long hours at your business usually isn't any better for the health of your company than it is for your own health.

Your thoughts will naturally drift to your business on Free-Thought Days. When ideas come to mind, write them down and then move on to doing a nonbusiness activity. You may inspire your creativity by doing things such as relaxing in a hot shower, taking a short nap, or getting in a good workout at the gym.

Science fiction writer Isaac Asimov was reported to cure his writer's block by going to the movies. Since some of Asimov's ideas have certainly been among the most creative of any writer, it seems safe to assume his approach worked. If one's conscious mind is busy with something that doesn't require deep concentration (like a movie), the subconscious mind is free to solve problems. While the conscious mind is busy, the creative juices flow, and ideas seem to come out of nowhere.

I use this "movie strategy" myself. I cannot count the number of times I have come up with solutions for a difficult problem while watching a movie. Movies and creativity really do work together.

Another option is to attend lectures or go someplace where you will be associating with non-work-related people who may embrace a different way of thinking from yours. The key word here is *different*. Spending time with people whose interests are different from yours gives you a chance to see things from a new perspective. This new and different perspective can often be the key to coming up with a new idea or creatively solving a problem.

Creativity Booster 4: Step outside Preconceived or Traditional Ideas

One business owner I know prematurely locks in on an early solution to problems and challenges based upon how she has viewed or handled similar situations in the past. She does not allow herself the time to look at other, possibly better, alternatives. You will free up your creativity if you do not lock in to solutions too soon.

The typical entrepreneurial nature is to try to implement ideas and changes as quickly as possible. But GEMs know that the best solutions result from taking time for conceptualization. If you are someone who habitually rushes to solve problems, one of your challenges will be to stop, take a deep breath, and consciously go through the creative steps presented in this chapter. This will allow you to avoid or neutralize the blocks normally brought on by your "rush" behavior.

In order to creatively solve certain challenges, you have to be able to deviate from the limited and automatic thinking that is locked into your brain. The likelihood of coming up with truly creative Strategies or Action Plans increases with the number of free-flowing ideas you can generate. This principle is often the key to solving the challenge.

A problem or challenge will often appear difficult or unsolvable because your assumptions about it are off base or even entirely wrong. To avoid this situation, try *lateral thinking*, which is a technique that involves looking at a given situation from unexpected angles in order to find a solution. Crossing out of your normal patterns of thought allows you to make connections with unrelated patterns and to develop new ideas.

Sometimes lateral thinking will carry you beyond the *logical* into what may appear to be too far outside the boundaries of the "box." Don't resist or automatically eliminate an idea because it appears too difficult or crazy to accomplish. In order to solve certain challenges, you have to be able to deviate from the limited and automatic thinking that is locked into your brain. GEMs are visionaries. They "think outside the box," or go beyond the norm, by deliberately avoiding the type of thinking that is limited to what has been done before.

Many people never even begin to take action because they automatically assume that if it has not already been done, it must be impossible to do. They have no faith in their ideas. In contrast, GEMs assume that their ideas will work. Can you imagine how many of the greatest business successes might never have taken place because something like it had never been done before, or because the risk seemed too great? I wonder what feedback Ray Kroc received when he told people he was going to franchise a fast-food restaurant called "McDonald's" or what people told

Steven Jobs when he said that Apple computer would be competing against the international giants.

The movie director Peter Weir, who had great success with the film *Witness*, also directed the movie *The Truman Show*. He was told by everyone that *The Truman Show* would bomb because the concept of people watching reality on television was too far-fetched to believe! *Survivor* came out two years later. Certainly everyone knows all too well how successful reality shows have become.

> **The fact that something has not already been done, or that other people have not succeeded in doing it in the past, should never be a reason not to do it.**

Soon after moving to the Aspen area, I befriended a doctor who told me that there is a reason why so many people have trouble thinking outside the box. He told me that it ties in with the cerebellum. The cerebellum (literally "little brain") is the part of the brain that orchestrates muscle action. Once the cerebral cortex (the part of the brain associated with higher brain function such as thought and action) orders a movement, the cerebellum automatically tells the muscles how to move.

As the doctor explained, based on certain information that is stored in the human brain, the cerebellum functions so that we automatically do many things without engaging in an actual thought process. This is a repetitive response that affects more than just physical movement—it is also a mental response. Most people never even get their creative juices flowing because of this automatic, habitual thinking that blocks their creative ideas. You have to fight this biological factor to become your most creative you.

While working on a building expansion, I was faced with a problem that existed due to a restraint relating to setback lines and the cost factor of moving a driveway to meet these restraints. After being told by both the builder and the architect on the project that there was no solution without getting a variance, I let my imagination go wild in search of a solution. Initially I used visual imagery in an abstract manner to come up with ideas. In other words, I let my mind go wild. Later, when my ideas were formulated, I used my rather poor sketching abilities to put my ideas on paper. These sketches resulted in several ideas for possible Strategies.

The first few Strategies that I came up with were not feasible. But eventually I came up with an idea that worked—without having to get a variance. It had the extra benefit of creating a more interesting looking building.

Why was I able to come up with a solution when my builder and architect could not? One advantage I certainly had over them was that I was not locked into the preconceived rules that had created rigidity in their thinking. They were relying on approaches they had used with success in the past while I, who had never been faced with a similar problem, was starting with a clean slate.

TAB facilitator-coach Steve Davis spoke to me about the experience of hiring a new employee who suddenly started accomplishing things the predecessor never had been able to do. He felt this happened because nobody told the new hire it was impossible to do so. This same principle explains why TAB members are able to solve problems for their fellow members. Each TAB Board is made up of members who come from noncompeting fields. This results in ideas that are not locked into the conventional thinking of the industry in which the member with the problem operates. As I have already mentioned, stepping outside your preconceived ideas is often the key to finding a solution.

GEMs rarely exclude ideas. Their minds are constantly alive and always yielding dividends. Dare to allow your mind to wander and leave it free to explore untraditional realms. Some seemingly outlandish ideas have been the foundations for many successful actions.

Creative thinking can be totally thrown off by something as simple as a phone call or someone's asking where a file is—basically, the simple distractions that business owners face daily. This is why much of your best conceptual thinking will take place when you are away from the office or from any distractions at your home. The great majority of my most successful creative ideas have taken place when I was doing something away from the office. Go someplace you enjoy and let your mind go free.

There is no fast and firm rule for conceptualization. In fact, we all conceptualize differently. One day after explaining to my daughter Michele how I had constructed certain imagery in my mind to solve a problem, she told me that she just could not conceptualize the same way I did. She needs to see things on paper to be able to conceptualize effectively while I can easily visualize things in my head. The key isn't how you conceptualize, but that you do conceptualize.

Creativity Booster 5: Make Notes while Ideas Are Still Fresh

TAB facilitator-coach Ray Brun told me that when ideas come to him during the night, he immediately gets up and writes himself a note. Doing this also helps him sleep better. "Once I know my idea is safely written down," Brun says, "I am free to go back to sleep."

GEMs have a common quirk: they constantly write notes to themselves or record thoughts about why something is not working and the possible changes they may want to make. Some stash these notes in shirt pockets and dictate them to an assistant later, as I do, while others methodically recopy them in some sense of order when they get an extra minute.

Putting your ideas down on paper gets them out of your mind and opens the mental space needed to consciously analyze all of your alternatives. It also opens your mind to new ideas that will result from the different aspects of what you have written. Creating written notes will help you keep the flow going so you are not locked in to the first idea you come up with. It will also prevent you from forgetting your good thoughts and ideas.

I have note pads by my bed, in my car, on my desk, at my conference table, and in my briefcase. You never know when you'll get an idea, so be prepared to write down or record your ideas whenever they occur. Above all, avoid being too brief in your notes. Jotting down one or two words may not be enough to retrigger your thoughts several hours or days later.

Allow your inner visionary to surface when making notes. Jot down any thoughts and ideas that come into your mind that give even the slightest possible solution to your problem—regardless of how crazy or impossible they may seem. Go in whatever direction your mind takes you, and refrain from making judgments about how valid your ideas are until later.

Give yourself the distance of a few hours or days from what you wrote and then review your notes. If you find an idea does not have enough merit to fly on its own, consider whether you may be able to take part of idea A and part of idea D and find a way to unite the two to create a viable solution. The most important thing is the consideration of all the ideas expressed in your notes and whether there is any value to them even if the ideas need to be modified or integrated.

Creativity Booster 6: Trust Your Instincts

Within months of starting with Tipton, I heard that the Kroger grocery store chain was moving out of a 23,000-square-foot prime location in a major regional shopping center. The information was discussed while at a meeting with executives of several large retail chains. The reaction of the others at the meeting was that the location would be ideal for their company but that Kroger had surely subleased the space to some other retailer if there was any significant time left on Kroger's lease.

Instead of dropping the matter as the others did, I contacted Kroger and found out that they had not yet made any arrangements for the space and that they had 10 years left on their lease at a rate factor that was substantially less than the current market rent for the location. I decided to fly to Cincinnati and meet with the top executives of Kroger. I offered a creative proposition in which Tipton would pay Kroger more than it was already paying in rent but which was significantly less than what I considered to be market value. This way both companies would benefit.

I mentioned my reasons for flying to Cincinnati to several of the Tipton executives, and I was told by one of them that monkeys would fly out of my ass before I got the sublease. I did get the sublease, and it made Tipton a substantial amount of money. Was I lucky to have succeeded? No! I decided to not simply assume that it could not be done.

Don't let others talk you out of your ideas if you believe they can bring about a Big Picture impact. Many great ideas would never have been carried out if the GEMs who thought of them had agreed with those who said, "It just can't be done," or "If it's really such a great idea, it would already have been done." Over the years, many business owners have told me of opportunities they have missed because they did not trust their instincts.

Many people, not just business owners, do not trust their instincts. If this is true of you, make a conscious effort to overcome this pattern by going with your instincts on less important matters at first. The experience of seeing the positive results from this will give you the confidence to use your instincts on bolder moves.

Creativity Booster 7: Analyze the Alternatives

Benjamin Franklin wrote that, "All reasons pro and con are not present to the mind at the same time . . ." His statement is true, and as a result of this fact, the mind, like a pendulum swinging back and forth, is influenced by whatever occurs to us at the time. This does not allow us to consider all the alternatives at once, thus keeping us from arriving at the best solution to the problem.

I rely on an analysis technique perfected by Benjamin Franklin that addresses just this situation. First, divide a sheet of paper into two columns. In one column list the Pros for each solution you have created, and in the other column list the Cons. As Franklin explained, "When each [pro and con reason] is thus considered separately and comparatively, and the whole lies before me, I think I judge better and am less likely to make a rash step . . ."

The visual assessment such a list provides will help you pinpoint the best direction to take in creatively solving the problem. Upon visually seeing the upside versus the downside of your alternative solutions, you will find that some of your ideas are just not practical or worth the risk although they may have been extremely exciting when they first floated through your mind. You will be able to determine which solutions have the greatest downside risk and reject those ideas, thereby narrowing your choices.

Creativity Booster 8: Tap into the Ideas of Others

With permission from her members, TAB facilitator-coach Barba Hickman met with the top employees of each of her members from one of the TAB Boards she facilitates. She confidentially asked them, "Imagine that when you come to work tomorrow, you find out that your CEO has been in a fatal accident and has legally left the company to you. What three things would you do differently to make sure the company was as successful as possible?"

The employees at first looked shocked at the question, but then they quickly became animated and enumerated great ideas. In each case, after Hickman shared what she learned with her members, each of them quickly instituted a brainstorming session with their top employees to discuss, and in many cases implement, their ideas.

Business owners can become so locked into their own views that they are not receptive to the creative ideas of their employees. Are you guilty of this behavior? Is the creative process among your management team members thwarted by your negative emotional response to potentially great ideas?

I like to inform my managers of my objective and then ask them for their ideas on how it can be accomplished. Sometimes I will do this at a meeting and then leave the room knowing my managers will hammer out the ideas among themselves. I do this to force them to use their creativity in coming up with ways to accomplish my objectives.

Some of the most creative ideas will come from the feedback of employees at the nonmanagement level. Employees at this level of your organization can often be particularly good at coming up with practical suggestions for solving problems that are keeping your Action Plans from working. The challenge is getting the ideas communicated to the right people. GEMs use many different combinations to open the lock on non-management-level employee ideas including brainstorming sessions, special committees of employees from all levels, and the old, but still very valuable, suggestion box.

GEMs express what they want done in a confident manner, but they do not close the door on others who wish to express thoughts and ideas that may ultimately result in better plans. Some of your most creative ideas may come from the suggestions of employees, family members, and others. Especially valuable are the ideas of those who are able to view the situation in a way you cannot and are thereby afforded the ability to come up with ideas and solutions of which you might not think. Keep yourself open to different, opposing, and/or out-of-the-box views, and never give the impression that your views are the only correct ones.

I am fortunate in that I spend some of my social time doing outdoor activities with friends who are also successful entrepreneurs. This allows me to hash out my problems in an informal and enjoyable setting while obtaining feedback from friends who are not locked into the structured thinking of my industry.

Most business owners are not as fortunate. This is one of the reasons I created The Alternative Board. Before forming TAB, I made the suggestion to several entrepreneurs that they put together an informal advisory group of business owners to help them solve their problems. Not one of them was able to effectively do this. After a few years of watching these failures, I realized how important the need was for an organization that could successfully form these "think tanks" for entrepreneurs.

Many TAB members have told me that their basic nature was never one that instinctively sought out advice from others. As a result of becoming a part of the TAB community, they admit to having learned the benefits of peer advice, and they now embrace the advice they receive from their fellow TAB Board members. The easy solution to getting help from group feedback is to attend a TAB Board meeting and let the other business-owner members—a highly experienced "think tank"—help you come up with creative solutions based on their many years of combined business experience.

The TAB think-tank atmosphere creates a safe space for ideas to be aired and allows creativity to flow. TAB assembles a collection of creative minds into each board that feed off of each other. This allows creative input to reach amazing levels. The result is an atmosphere in which all members milk the positive aspects from every idea conceived.

Creativity Checklist

• Overcome the time obstacles that keep you from developing your creative skills.

- Look at a major task from the perspective of how and when you must accomplish every phase of the process, and create a detailed schedule that breaks down the steps involved.
- Create a things-to-do list.
- Don't reinvent the wheel; learn what others in similar situations have done.
- Learn to say no in order to open up needed time.
- Stop partaking in nonemergency, nonbusiness phone calls during work hours.
- Schedule your availability to employees so it does not distract you from focusing on reaching your dreams.
- Delegate!
- Don't waste time on the past.
- Identify the real challenge or the real problem.
- Do your homework to stay abreast of what others are doing to create their success.
- Access your creative juices by not thinking about the problem for a while.
- Allow your mind to wander and explore untraditional realms.
- Make notes!
- Find ways to integrate your thoughts.
- Trust your instincts.
- Analyze your alternatives.
- Be open to the feedback of others.

CHAPTER 7

THE SECRET OF
CHANGING COURSE

Regardless of how well you construct your plans and how hard you try to make them happen, you may find that some things still don't go the way you want. This does not mean failure. It means that you have to make course changes. GEMs know that things will not always go as planned, and they recognize the need to execute smooth course changes in order to achieve the dreams of their Personal Vision.

There are two key elements to successfully changing course. The first element involves scheduling time on a regular basis to review and revise your Personal Vision Statement, SWOT Statements, and Personal Plans. The second element involves identifying and overcoming the roadblocks to successful course changes. The Secret of Changing Course is an ongoing process; there is no stopping point. Let's take a look at the review and revise process; the first step of changing course.

Reviewing and Revising Your Personal Vision Statement

In the months leading up to my fortieth birthday, I spent many hours soul-searching for what I wanted to do with the "rest of my life," just as many people do. I found that the dreams that made up my Personal Vision Statement included business-related things such as Tipton's becoming a publicly owned company or my being able to generate a specific minimum amount of money by selling my Tipton stock. My dreams also included nonbusiness things such as one day having a home in the mountains. I recognized that I had far too much self-imposed stress in my life and that I wanted a more balanced lifestyle.

At age 45, after Tipton was sold and I had moved to the Aspen, Colorado, area, my Personal Vision Statement changed. It reflected new desires such as sharing my business experiences by writing a syndicated column and lecturing. I was no longer actively involved in the day-to-day activities of running a business, and at that time I had no plans to start another business.

Just three years later my Personal Vision Statement changed again when I became excited about starting The Alternative Board. I revised my Personal Vision Statement to reflect my desired involvement with TAB and to detail the impact I wanted the company to have upon my life. My Personal Vision included points such as remaining the CEO of TAB as long as my family owned the company but eventually giving up my chief operating officer role.

I specified the time involvement I desired both inside and outside the company. This factor included designating four days a week as Free-Thought Time—that is, days when I did not want to be contacted by anyone at TAB unless it was an emergency. I included the financial benefits I wanted from TAB and the fact that I wanted TAB to become an internationally important source of help to business owners. This last factor was especially meaningful to me from a psychic standpoint. My Personal Vision Statement also expressed my desire to build TAB to a level at which the potential would exist for it to either become a publicly owned company or be sold for a specific minimum amount of money.

My desire to either go public or sell the company changed after my daughter Lynette married Jason Zickerman. After Jason proved himself to be an exceptional president and COO of TAB, I revised my Personal Vision Statement to match a new desire to keep TAB ownership in the family. Because I found that I enjoyed my daily mentoring interaction with Jason, I also revised my Personal Vision Statement to eliminate the four days I had previously designated as Free-Thought Time. I replaced this with my desire to be available to Jason whenever he wanted to discuss TAB matters.

Even though your Personal Vision Statement is likely to remain relatively constant for several years at a time, you can see from my experience that you will need to make changes as your life changes. At TAB, we recommend that our members review their Personal Vision Statements once a month and that they revise these statements to accommodate any changes that have occurred in their lives if necessary.

During your monthly review, look at what has taken place in your life since the last time you reviewed and revised your Personal Vision Statement, or since you wrote it if this is your first time reviewing and revising. Ask yourself if any changes have occurred that are significant enough to warrant a revision or course change to any part of your Personal Vision Statement. You may find that your Personal Vision is no longer realistically achievable based on the realities of your current life.

Revisions often need to be made because something wonderful has occurred such as the birth of a child or grandchild. When I became a grandfather, my Personal Vision changed to include spending a lot of time with my grandchildren. Unfortunately, negative factors can also be the cause for needed revisions to your Personal Vision Statement. One business owner had a Personal Vision Statement that included a retirement dream of extensive international travel with his wife. A lifelong habit of heavy smoking caused him to develop health problems. He was forced to make drastic revisions to his Personal Vision Statement because he was no longer able to travel on airplanes due to the oxygen tank he then had to carry to help him breathe.

If you lose passion for any part of your Personal Vision Statement, you will probably never see it achieved. The discovery of a new opportunity can engage a new passion that may cause you to lose interest in another. You may need to make changes to your Personal Vision Statement to reflect your changed passions. A renewed passion for horses and trail riding was cause for definite changes to certain aspects of my Personal Vision Statement.

> **Even if there are no changes that need to be made, taking the time to do the monthly review and revision of your Personal Vision Statement will always be worthwhile because the review will help keep your sights focused on your long-range dreams.**

Reviewing and Revising Your Personal SWOT Statements

Years ago I was in a taxicab accident that injured my lower back. Due to my injury I was forced to make changes to my written Weaknesses Statement. I could no longer ski the bumps with friends or take long hikes with a heavy backpack. I also had to factor time into my daily schedule for stretching exercises.

At TAB, we recommend that members review their SWOT Statements each month during the same time they review their Personal Vision Statements. Unlike your Personal Vision Statement, your Personal SWOT Statements will require changes fairly often. Review your SWOT Statements in the same order that you created them: strengths, weaknesses, opportunities, and threats.

Ask yourself what changes have taken place that might result in making a revision to your Personal Competitive Edge Strengths Statement. One business owner added business financing to his Strengths Statement after successfully arranging a loan for his manufacturing company. Another business owner's Competitive Edge Strengths Statement originally included negotiating as one of her strengths. She revised her Strengths Statement and removed negotiating from it after having an experience in which she did a poor job negotiating.

Next review your Weaknesses Statement. Since your last review, have you neutralized any weaknesses listed in your Weaknesses Statement? One business owner's Weaknesses Statement listed a weakness in human resources matters. After attending a workshop on hiring and firing and gaining experience in many different HR situations over a few years' time, he felt he had neutralized this weakness, and he removed it from his Weaknesses Statement.

Sometimes you may identify a weakness that you did not previously realize existed. It often takes a while to recognize all of our weaknesses. During a meeting with the executive vice president of a service company, the vice president mentioned that the owner of the company came across to his employees as being arrogant. When I asked the vice president to explain, he said that the owner habitually put down other people's ideas and any changes they suggested.

I met with the business owner over dinner a short time later. He brought up a concern that some of his plans were not getting the projected results. I questioned whether this was due to the fact that his employees perceived him as being arrogant. He said he was not aware that he was perceived by his employees in this way. He admitted that he had difficulty accepting others' ideas and that this was due to the lack of recognition and attention he had received while growing up. This explained, although it did not excuse, his behavior. I mentioned that even the perception by others that he possessed these characteristics may be stopping those he needed most from giving him the full support he needed to get what he wanted. Later that month during the review of his Weaknesses Statement he revised it by adding "Perceived by others as being arrogant."

When things do not go as planned, the natural inclination for most people is to search for an external reason, when instead, they should be taking a closer look in their personal mirror to uncover the root cause of the problem. What are you doing that might be contributing to the less-than-optimal outcome you're getting? All too often we are our own worst enemy. Even though it is hard to acknowledge our weaknesses, looking for previously unidentified personal weaknesses may be the linchpin to making course changes that will get you where you want to go.

Next ask what changes have taken place that may alter your written Opportunities Statement. One business owner's Opportunities Statement listed the opportunity to bring his son into his service company. After his son joined the business, he removed this opportunity from his Opportunities Statement.

Finally, look at factors that may alter your written Threats Statement. One business owner listed the threat of his CFO's health since the man had experienced and recovered from a stroke. Unfortunately, another stroke occurred and the CFO died. This threat obviously came off his written Threats Statement.

Divorce, death, and illnesses are all elements that may result in your having to make revisions to your SWOT Statements. The fact that you don't have control over all pain and suffering should not lead you to take the view that happiness is impossible to achieve. As my mom often says, "Life is not perfect, so go with the flow."

After making revisions to your SWOT Statements, it is very common to have to make revisions to your Personal Vision Statement.

Reviewing and Revising Your Personal Plans

Your written Personal Plans are likely to encounter frequent changes. If the results you are getting for your Personal Plans are not what you want, ask yourself why the desired results are not taking place. Then determine what changes need to be made to your Personal Plans in order to reach your desired destination. Critical Success Factors, Goals, Strategies, and Action Plans should never be viewed as static. It is necessary to review these four elements in each of your Personal Plan Statements.

The most common reason to revise a CSF is because you have changed some element in your Personal Vision Statement or you have revised your SWOT Statements. One real estate developer had a Personal Vision that included selling his business and relocating with his wife to Nevada. This was the CSF of one of his Personal Plans. After his wife left him for another man, he revised his Personal Vision Statement and changed the CSF of his Personal Plan. He did sell his business and relocate. But instead of going to Nevada, he sold his home and downsized to a smaller home in the same general area in which he had been living.

You may find that a Goal is no longer realistically attainable. This may require major changes to your Goals Statement. One business owner had a Goal of working no more than four days a week by the end of the year. He revised the Goal to reflect working four and a half days because he realized it was just not feasible to take that much time away from the business if he wanted his company to attain its growth objectives.

In 2005 I reviewed a Personal Plan that had a Goal stating that within two years I would develop an advanced training program for facilitators of The Alternative Board. During the review I asked myself if I was being realistic with respect to creating this program in the given time frame while still maintaining the life balance I desired. My answer resulted in changing the Goal of my Personal Plan so I would complete only the most important topics of the advanced training program within three years.

Carol Crawford, a TAB facilitator-coach in Grand Rapids, Michigan, warns that business owners should be careful about changing Goals too impulsively. She says, "Not achieving a Goal by the established dates does not mean that you should change, adjust, or eliminate the Goal. Instead, you may want to simply change the expectation date for achieving the Goal." This is what I did relating to my plan for the advanced training program. At other times you will have no alternative but to make much more involved changes to your Goals.

Next, review, challenge, and possibly revise the Strategies for your Personal Plans. One business owner had a Goal in his Personal Plan to start a second business. One of his Strategies was to travel to several cities to research how other companies provided the same services he wanted the new business to offer. After several months he realized he did not have the time to make this Strategy work. He revised his Strategy to include engaging a marketing company to do a study of what other companies were doing in the type of service business in which he was interested.

The easiest part of your Personal Plans to review will be your Action Plans. Since Action Plans have timelines, it is easy to see if the benchmark results are being met. The results you envisioned when you made your Action Plans will not always turn out as expected. Don't allow yourself to obsess or mope if you have not made the progress for which you had hoped. Look at your mistakes and try to understand what went wrong. Your mistakes can be valuable learning tools. Your greatest asset in making effective course changes often comes from identifying why the desired results have not occurred and making changes to your Action Plans as needed.

Eliminating Personal Plans

When my son-in-law Jason and I decided that he would come into TAB with the ultimate objective of his being made president of the company, one of my Personal Plans included a Goal of becoming more involved in the day-to-day matters at TAB during a three-year mentoring period. I would then, at the end of the three years, eliminate as much as possible my hands-on time with TAB. This Personal Plan was achieved, and so I removed it from my active plans.

Ideally you will eliminate Personal Plans because the Goals of your Personal Plans have been achieved. Sometimes, however, you will remove them because your Goals cannot be achieved. During one coaching session with a business owner, I asked him how his Personal Plan for grooming his son to take over the day-to-day operations of his company was proceeding. He explained that his son had recently quit the family business to take an out-of-town job. The CSF of his Personal Plan disappeared when his son left the business. That Personal Plan was "canned."

Don't forget to let those who are affected by your Personal Plans know that you have eliminated a plan. In 2004 one of my first cousins died and another first cousin was battling bone cancer. These factors caused me to eliminate one of my Personal Plans. I sent the following e-mail to my key executives at TAB detailing my decision to eliminate a Personal Plan:

> Several months ago a first cousin of mine, who was only a few months younger than me, died of prostate cancer. Little more than three months ago, another first cousin of mine, whom I had been quite close to when we were younger, was diagnosed with bone cancer. She is currently undergoing her second series of chemotherapy and apparently there is no cure for her illness at this time.

These tragedies have resulted in causing me to rethink how I really want to be using my time as it pertains to TAB. I have decided that I do not want to dedicate the time necessary for my personal involvement in working on the potential strategic alliance between TAB and Company X.

Changes to your Personal Vision Statement may cause a Critical Success Factor to no longer be critical to achieving your dreams. This in turn may result in the elimination of an entire Personal Plan. Other times you will find that you need to focus more on certain Personal Plans and do not have the time to focus on all the Personal Plans you have developed.

As I was approaching my fortieth birthday, I revisited my Personal Vision Statement. During the review it became clear to me that I had to eliminate one or more of my Personal Plans in order to focus on the plans that were more important to accomplishing my Personal Vision Statement. I had to make a decision about what was most important to me, and this resulted in eliminating a Personal Plan for my involvement in political and government matters. As much as this political involvement interested me, the time required for it was substantial and could be better used to focus in on accomplishing Personal Plans that were more important to my attaining my Personal Vision.

Adding Personal Plans

When I designed the original TAB franchise model, I structured it so that franchisees paid a royalty to TAB based on a percentage of all the TAB membership income generated by the franchise. Under the royalty percentage model, TAB franchisees with outstanding membership results were not earning as much income as they could have been earning if they had been paying a flat fee to The Alternative Board.

I created a new Personal Plan to change the TAB franchise model to one in which The Alternative Board's income from franchisees would be a flat amount per territory called an "opportunity fee." The opportunity fee replaced the royalty percentage income in the old franchise model. I felt that the revised franchise opportunity model would result in a great leap forward for TAB in part because it would show much greater earnings potential to anyone thinking about buying a TAB franchise; and it did.

After you have your first Personal Plan off the ground and running, you will probably want to add additional Personal Plans. When adding your next Personal Plan, ask yourself which CSF has the greatest likelihood of bringing about a great leap forward for your personal life or business. Make this the CSF for your new Personal Plan.

Always add new Personal Plans one at a time, and never have more than five Personal Plans going at once. The fewer Personal Plans you are working on at one time, the more likely it is that you will accomplish them. I have coached people who were making great strides in accomplishing their Personal Plans when they were focusing on only two or three Personal Plans at a time. When they added additional Personal Plans, it caused them to lose their focus, and their results dropped off significantly.

When you feel ready to add a new Personal Plan, create it in the same way you created your first Personal Plan—by identifying your CSF, Goal, Strategies, and Action Plans.

Scheduling Weekly Reviews of Personal Plans

At TAB we recommend that members set aside a time each week for their weekly Personal Plan review. Your review should be scheduled for the same day and time each week, such as every Wednesday at 8 A.M. The key is scheduling uninterrupted time of no more than an hour or two for each review session. I personally find it easier to do this review away from the distractions of the office.

We give TAB members the option of using an electronic software package that we developed for tracking and revising Personal Plans or using a paper or off-the-shelf electronic tool for tracking results. The key is to use the tool that best fits your personality and style.

Overcoming Roadblocks to Course Changes

There are definite roadblocks that keep many business owners from reaping the full results of course changes. Unless you recognize and address these roadblocks, you will likely find yourself continually falling short of your dreams. GEMs acknowledge the roadblocks that exist on their journey to success and find ways to circumvent or clear these barriers. The following are six roadblocks that business owners commonly encounter while making course changes. Identify any roadblocks that are getting in the way of your course changes, and do what is needed to circumvent or eliminate them.

Roadblock 1: Inability to Admit Mistakes

One computer software company had already spent over $800,000 developing a new computer software program and was continuing to pour money into improving the product. The continued cost of product development was harming the company's cash flow because no sales of the new program were taking place. Except for the president of the company, who was the majority stockholder and who had conceived of the idea for the software program, everyone could see that the software package was going nowhere and that it would never attain high sales. The software program had become a Sacred Cow.

Over the objections of his employees, including the minority stockholders, the company president poured even more of the company's money and human resources into improving the software product. This was money and employee effort that should have been put toward updating and improving company products that were selling. The owner's inability to admit his mistake and stop pouring company resources into the software product that had become his "baby" was the major factor behind the company's ultimate failure.

The Sacred Cow syndrome involves continuing with a plan, or part of a plan, because the person who created the plan will not admit to having made a mistake. Continuing to invest in a Sacred Cow that does not make good business sense often sucks energy, cash, and profits from a company. In the example above, the company president clearly should have admitted his mistake and executed a course change.

In contrast, take a look at how the owner of a food production company handled a similar problem. The owner had created a new cookie product that was losing a large sum of money for his company. In spite of this fact, another company that had greater distribution capabilities had expressed an interest in buying the product.

Several of the company's executives recommended selling off the assets of the new cookie product. The owner of the company admitted his mistake and approved the sale. He did not allow the cookie product, which had also been his "baby," to become a Sacred Cow. The sale of the product cut off large losses and provided some proceeds that were used toward promoting several exciting new products. Admitting his mistake and making the right follow-up decisions eliminated a potential roadblock to a needed course change.

We all make mistakes and have failures. How these mistakes are acknowledged and handled is a major factor that separates GEMs from business owners who never reach the same level of success. GEMs admit when they are wrong and then move on to do whatever is needed to correct the problem. They don't allow their mistakes to become Sacred Cow roadblocks to course changes. GEMs typically employ the simple phrase "I'm wrong" and then move on. This two-word phrase is one of the most difficult things for some people to say, yet admitting you are wrong can often work wonders.

Many business owners have a problem admitting their mistakes because they think that such an admission will take away from the respect others, whether employees, family members, or friends, have for them. GEMs know that others will respect you more, and emulate your example, when you readily admit your mistakes and move forward.

Roadblock 2: Resistance to Course Changes

When TAB President and COO Jason Zickerman and I first introduced the course change of the new model for the TAB franchise opportunity, which I mentioned earlier, there was one TAB planning team member, a talented person whose advice I respect, who resisted this course change. Simply put, he was frightened of change and wanted to keep the status quo. His resistance was out of true concern based on his view of what was good for the company rather than a desire to intentionally hurt the company.

Unfortunately, he continued to openly fight the course change even after the decision was made to move ahead with the new model. Several planning team members informed me that he was trying to sway their thinking by telling them that disastrous results would take place if TAB changed to the new model. He lobbied the others on the planning team to try to convince Jason to get me to change my mind about implementing the new model changes. Some of the planning team members were influenced by his expressions of fear and became concerned.

Jason and I did not let resistance to change become a roadblock to making the needed course change. It took a concerted effort to neutralize the concerns created by the resistance efforts of this one person, but we took the needed steps to get the emotional buy-in of everyone whose commitment was critical to making the course change happen. The Alternative Board successfully executed the course change of going to a flat opportunity fee. Within one year of offering the new franchise opportunity, TAB brought on almost three times as many new territories as the year before.

Course changes can be a scary prospect for many people, especially when the changes are directed at the way things have always been done. It is not uncommon for executives or other employees to attempt to slow down or even outright stop your course changes. Those who attempt to spread fear and doubt about course changes among fellow employees, especially among those whose participation is needed to make your course changes happen, can present very real roadblocks to success. This holds equally true for family members and friends. Family members may go to the point of lobbying other family members against changes that are part of your nonbusiness course changes.

Resistance to course changes can create an enormous challenge to gaining the support you need to make your course changes happen. GEMs recognize that there is a line that separates constructive challenges to course changes and that of blatant resistance to change. GEMs meet blatant resistance head-on and make it clear to the person who is resisting, and who may be inciting the concerns and resistance of others, that the resistance must stop immediately. They also make the effort to sell the benefits of the course change to anyone who may have been influenced by the party resisting the change.

The course changes you implement must get some level of positive results within a matter of months of putting the changes into effect, or support for your course changes may wane or disappear altogether. I call this period the "honeymoon period." Showing some positive results during the honeymoon period will reinforce belief in the changes both by those who resisted the course change as well as by those who may have been influenced by the party or parties resisting the change.

It took me a couple of honeymoon periods before I figured out that the key to making sure the roadblock of resistance was kept out of the way was to show that some level of positive results had taken place with clear benchmarks during short intervals. Communicating recognition when short-term results are attained will sustain motivation in those who were doubters and those who are crucial to making your course changes happen.

Roadblock 3: Procrastination

During one TAB Board meeting, a member who owned a manufacturing company told me that his Personal Plan for buying a vacation home was not going to be achieved that year because of production problems. The cash flow he needed for the vacation home was dependent on good company results, and his results had been disappointing. He blamed the production problems on an operations manager who was obsessively "hands on." The owner felt that the man's management style was a bottleneck to the company and that he was responsible for the cause of numerous delays and setbacks.

The business owner felt that making a course change to remove the operations manager from his current position would be difficult to do since the man had started with the company when it had only a handful of employees. He stated that the operations manager was a loyal and hard-working employee but that he was not adept at delegating. This problem had become more and more apparent as the company grew to include more employees.

The business owner told me how one of his company draftsmen had recently come to him complaining that the operations manager had demanded to see the first draft of a certain set of drawings. The drawings had been left sitting untouched on the operation manager's desk for weeks because he was too busy to look at them. The delay in reviewing the drawings resulted in setting back the production schedule by several weeks. When questioned by the owner about this situation, the operations manager explained that the only way he could have the control he needed to get the job done right was to require that all employees who reported to him keep him apprised of everything that was happening in the department.

After a lot of prodding from his fellow TAB Board members, the TAB member overcame his roadblock of procrastination and made the needed course change. He finally told the operations manager that his hands-on policy and production delays would no longer be accepted. The operations manager got the message that he needed to change his ways, but he just could not do it. It wasn't who he was. After several months had passed without the needed results taking place, the owner hired a new operations manager. He transferred the previous operations manager to a parallel-level job that did not involve management skills.

The business owner should have addressed the problem years earlier when the operations manager first started having difficulty managing a greater number of people. He allowed the roadblock of procrastination to keep him from making a needed course change.

Many entrepreneurs fail to become GEMs because of paralysis by analysis. They endlessly think about or discuss what needs to be done and never actually make a move. In contrast, GEMs don't overanalyze. There comes a time when you have to stop analyzing and act. It is rare to have all the facts you would like before you take action. GEMs use their best judgment, trust their instincts, and make the Seven Secrets a part of their everyday life.

Are there course changes that you know need to be made but that you put off or avoid doing altogether in hopes that the need for the change will go away? Procrastination can be deadly to the growth of your business and to your happiness in general. GEMs take a proactive approach to making course changes by removing the barrier of procrastination and making the needed course changes when they need to be made.

Another TAB Board member shared with his TAB Board his struggles with chronic procrastination when it came to making needed course changes. His fellow TAB Board members recommended that he engage a particular business psychology group to find out why he procrastinated in these situations. It turned out that the business owner was a perfectionist. He did not want to make any changes until he felt he knew the best way to make the changes. Consequently, any project on which he doubted his ability to succeed to his satisfaction resulted in procrastinating about making the needed course changes.

Many business owners have a terrible habit of procrastinating when it comes to making the changes necessary for reaching greater success. Before you can break your tendency toward procrastination, you need to understand why you procrastinate. If chronic procrastination is one of your roadblocks to making timely course changes, break down the reasons behind it. What is it about making a decision that causes dread on your part?

Many people misread the causes of procrastination and think the problem exists because of laziness. Most times it is not a matter of laziness, nor is it due to being unaware that course changes need to take place. Some of the hardest-working business owners have the greatest problems with overcoming the roadblock of chronic procrastination when it comes to course changes. As in the case of the TAB member above who is a perfectionist, the reason why most people procrastinate is typically not due to lack of intelligence or hard work.

While sharing a ski lift with a friend of mine who owns a very successful business, he told me that early in his career he often took too long to make the changes his company needed. My friend, who is exceptionally bright, said that when he was younger, he overanalyzed every situation before making any decisions, thus frustrating his subordinates and not capitalizing on opportunities. He was always overworked and stressed because of the time it took him to make decisions. He was also constantly late in making the changes needed to propel him toward success at a much faster rate. At a certain point he decided that he just had to go with his gut on some needed changes and stop overanalyzing things. It is not coincidental that this is when his company started its great leap forward.

GEMs make course changes in a timely manner, and they react faster, with more flexibility and aggression, than their competition. GEMs know that a decision made too late can be just as bad as a wrong decision. They establish realistic deadlines for making their course changes and then do what is necessary to get the needed results. Business owners who allow the roadblock of procrastination to keep them from making course changes in a timely manner will never be effective leaders nor will they be likely to reach the happiness and success they desire.

GEMs understand that it is their responsibility to make course changing decisions. Don't put this responsibility off. Work on changing any subconscious resistance roadblocks you have to making decisions. Close your eyes and see yourself getting your facts, weighing them, and acting on them. Don't allow yourself to put off the course changes that need to be made.

> **A side benefit of breaking the roadblock of chronic procrastination is that it will reduce your stress and anxiety levels. The longer you avoid a course change that needs to be addressed, the more your anxiety about it will build up.**

Roadblock 4: Fear of Making Bold Moves

The owner of a distribution-service company, whom I will call John, saw an opportunity to expand his business into a city that was only 250 miles away. The expansion would allow him to take advantage of a vacuum that existed in the city for a company that provided his company's products. John considered revising the Personal Plans for his company in order to take advantage of expanding into the second city, but he decided against making this bold move. He feared the newly added overhead in doing the expansion might negatively affect the amount of compensation he paid himself out of his business if the second location did not become profitable by the second year of operation.

John passed on an opportunity to make a course change that could bring him greater success and happiness because he was afraid of making a bold move. Not long after John passed on this opportunity, a company similar to John's that was based in a city much farther away opened in the second city. Once that company became successful in the second city, it then opened up in the city where John's company was located, and it became a very strong competitor for him. This new competition was one of the key factors in eventually putting John's company out of business.

Allowing roadblocks created from a fear of making bold moves often leads to failure. One second-generation-owned business that sold parts out of a single location in a large city had been successful for several decades. The owner's problems started when new technology allowed out-of-town companies that had once been suppliers to his company to sell the same products directly to customers in his town.

These out-of-town, Web-based companies competed without the same brick-and-mortar expenses that his company had. This allowed them to offer the same goods for lower prices. The business owner looked at several alternative course changes he could make to address the problem, but each of the changes required making a bold move. So he elected to "play it safe," as he stated, and did not make any course changes at all. His company was ultimately forced to liquidate.

GEMs are not reluctant to make course changes that require bold moves. When Jason and I saw an opportunity to greatly increase the number of TAB's franchised offices, we decided that first we needed to develop a much greater infrastructure to handle the desired expansion. The increased infrastructure required an increase in human resources, new and improved marketing materials, and new technology all before we could sell additional TAB franchises. There were some people within the company who felt we should prove that we could sell the new franchises before we focused the money on the improved infrastructure.

Expanding the infrastructure required making a bold move. It involved a substantial money commitment without any guarantee of increasing the number of franchised offices. Our bold move resulted in success levels for the new franchise territories that could not have taken place without the additional support that was available from the increased infrastructure.

GEMs push aside any roadblocks that stem from a fear of failure. There is a big difference between taking the attitude of "I think I can do something" and having the confidence to say "I will get it done." GEMs change course when they feel confident that the course change will get the desired results. Of course, it does not need to be said that there is never a guarantee that failure is not a possibility.

The owner of one retail shoe store that carried midpriced to high-end priced types of shoes faced the challenge of having a national retail chain open a large store nearby. The chain sold some of the same highly recognizable brand-name shoes. Some of the owner's employees expressed the view that the smaller company was doomed. The owner knew that she needed to make a bold move or she would eventually go out of business.

After looking at many course change options, she decided to add a dimension to her business that differentiated her from the big chain. She invested the money to buy equipment to make custom orthotics and to train her sales staff in comfort fitting. She did not allow the fear of making a bold move to be a roadblock that would stop her from taking a calculated risk. She was not a quitter. She made the bold move rather than stopping at the "can'ts" and "if onlys." She turned them into "why nots" and "do its." Her business became more successful than ever, and within a couple of years it expanded into the space next to her store.

Without taking at least some risks, a company will usually make very little true progress. Many business owners take the attitude of "I won't have to worry about failing if I don't take any risks," thereby passing up the chance for increased success. Some of the most talented, brightest, and best-educated business owners have not made the bold moves that could have taken their companies to their potential because they feared the possibility of failure. In contrast, GEMs educate themselves on the factors involved in the risks they are considering. Typically GEMs act on only those risks that show an upside potential benefit that is substantially greater than the downside impact.

I find that business owners are often more willing to make bold moves when they feel they have less to lose if they fail. This is typically when a business is just starting out. The longer a company has been established, the more often I see business owners being blocked from bold action by the fear that a bold course change will not work.

It may seem ironic, but this is an area where you should take a cue from small children. If you have ever skied, you have no doubt noticed that children who are three or four years old can ski almost immediately upon being put up on skis. They have no fear of falling—or failing. The first time I took my granddaughter on the slopes and talked to her about falling, she offhandedly said to me, "If I fall, I fall." Applying the same type of attitude that my granddaughter did toward falling to your decision-making process will help you make course changes that can make the difference between success and failure.

Remember when you were a kid and you went through the ritual of learning to ride a two-wheeler? You probably fell a lot. Falling may seem to be a failure, but is it really? Learning to avoid the fall is really incentive to learn to ride. If your parents had run after you and caught you every time you started to fall, you never would have learned how to reestablish your balance. If they had kept you from suffering the consequences of your mistakes, you may never have learned how to handle the bike.

Too many business owners have a fear of taking bold course changes when things get tough. In contrast, the "buck stops" with GEMs because they are the ones who assume the responsibility for their own success. When their paths appear to be blocked, GEMs take charge of the situation and keep fighting by making bold course changes. This doesn't mean they rush in like a bull in a china shop. What it means is that they don't let the fear of failure become a roadblock.

> **The same boldness in putting aside the fear of failure applies in your nonbusiness life. In life we all are faced with factors beyond our control. Those who are afraid to take bold moves rarely reach the success of their dreams.**

Roadblock 5: Not Knowing What You Don't Know

One new TAB member shared with his fellow board members the fact that three years earlier he had made a course change in which he left a large, well-known custom-software provider in order to use one that provided a "lowest-priced" customized system for his company. The lowest-priced company had since dissolved, and there was no one available to support his business software. He could not even bring in a new provider to run the old system as there were documented codes for the software that the member did not own or have access to.

One of his fellow TAB Board members mentioned that it was a shame that the new member had not been on the TAB Board at the time he made this ill-fated course change. He said the board would have strongly advised him against going with the lowest-priced company due to a similar bad experience he'd had some time ago because his software wasn't documented. The member said he would have gladly shared this experience with the new member as evidence as to why his course change was a bad idea.

The new member made a major mistake with his course change because of the roadblock of not knowing what he did not know. The fact is that no matter how experienced we are as business owners, there are going to be areas where we don't know what we don't know. The sooner that you accept this fact, the sooner you will be able to get around this roadblock and change course more effectively.

GEMs know that it is an enormous advantage to get advice from those who know what it is like to be at the top. Once you are made aware of the fact that you don't know something, you can eliminate the roadblock by finding the solution to what you do not know. If you don't recognize that there is a potential problem, then you won't actively look for the answers to the problem. This makes the roadblock of not knowing what you don't know especially hazardous to success.

A TAB Board member of TAB facilitator-coach John Dini discussed with his TAB Board a plan to set up a new division of his company. The new division would supply a different product but one that was related to the products already sold by his company. A few months later he stated that he was thinking of changing course and not setting up a company-owned division. He said he was interested in forming a new company that would be a joint venture with the man he had considered hiring to head up the new division. He explained to his TAB Board that the potential joint venture would involve his contribution of the capital and distribution capability and the other party was to contribute the personal skills and contacts.

He stated that one of his reasons for the course change was that he had concerns about the other man's professionalism and dependability. The member explained that by setting up a joint-venture company that would be legally separate from his business, he could reduce the potential negative exposure to his company if something went wrong with the new business.

Certain members of the TAB Board challenged whether his concerns about hiring the other man were not flags that should make him question whether he should be entering into a joint-venture relationship with this party. One member shared her own experience with the distraction of a joint venture that pulled her attention away from her primary business. Another member talked about a similar type of investment he had made in a joint venture and the agony of deciding whether to invest more or let it fail when it started to fall apart.

After listening to the shared experiences and counsel of his peers, the member decided not to make the course change of entering into the joint venture. Instead, he changed his course to one that involved setting up a new corporation in which he kept 100 percent of the ownership. His new plan included recruiting someone with experience to run the new corporation in whom he could have complete confidence. It took him several months to accomplish this, but the course change worked successfully.

Interestingly, several months after the board convinced him not to go into a joint venture, the member shared how the party with whom he had considered doing the joint venture had gone on to fail in another situation. The member did not make the course change because of the advice of his TAB Board. This decision saved him many wasted hours and unnecessary diversions from focusing on his core business.

David Halpern, chief innovative officer of TAB and a TAB facilitator-coach in Denver, Colorado, facilitated a meeting in which a member mentioned that he had used several of the residents who lived in his buildings to do repair and maintenance work on the buildings in which they lived. He stated that he paid them a lot less than the professional construction companies he had been using and that his plan was to change from using professional construction companies to using tenants in his building to do repairs and maintenance. An attorney on the board asked whether he had covered these tenants with worker's compensation. The attorney pointed out the exposure that could jeopardize the other member's entire business. The member who owned the buildings was astounded and responded, "I had no idea that I needed to get them covered by worker's compensation."

GEMs don't let themselves get stopped by the roadblock of things they do not know. They have trusted peers and/or a coach to meet with at a regularly scheduled time each month, and they seek advice from their peers who are fellow business owners who have been there and done it to check out their ideas and plans to make sure there are no potential problems of which they were not aware.

Roadblock 6: Lack of Personal Accountability

TAB facilitator-coach David Halpern shared another story in which a mortgage broker told his fellow TAB Board members that he was changing his plan. His course change was to go from being the sole employee responsible for sales to a plan in which he was going to bring on additional salespeople. The new plan started with the hiring of one salesperson and would lead up to eventually hiring two more salespeople. He told the board that hiring the first salesperson was going to be his top priority for the next month.

A month later, at the next TAB Board meeting, when the board members asked him how many potential sales employees he had interviewed, he responded with a stutter saying, "None." He had many excuses such as not having the time, but his fellow board members pressed him to answer why he was not being account-able to his course change. They recounted the reasons he had given the previous month of why this had to be his priority. One member reminded him that he needed to get this course change done to reach the Personal Vision he had shared with the board of spending less time on work activities.

At the next month's meeting, the member reported that he had interviewed many salesperson prospects and that he had hired his first salesperson. He added, with a smile, that he would have been too embarrassed to show up at the meeting without having met the commitment that he had made to himself and had also shared with the board.

Business owners are not routinely accountable to anyone. So a peer board, such as The Alternative Board, and a coach, such as a TAB facilitator-coach, helps keep business owners accountable for their plans. The TAB Board and TAB facilitator-coach ask about and discuss the progress that the business owner is making and help to implement course changes as needed. TAB Board members provide an external source of accountability for one another, and they provide experienced advice to help one another realize the dreams of what they want in life and in business.

One business owner asked his CPA, his attorney, and the fi-nancial planner for his business to be on his advisory board. The people he chose were not effective in providing him with ac-countability because all three were beholden to him for their jobs. They could not be objective without risking that what they said might result in being fired. Never have an employee or a profes-sional whom your company engages serve on an advisory team that helps review and revise your plans and course changes. To get real benefit, your advisors must have nothing to lose in speaking honestly to you.

Advisors cannot be truly effective without understanding the why behind each part of your plans. This means you must be truly honest and completely open with them. TAB Board members share their written Statements with their fellow TAB Board members. Confiding in someone who is competing with you offers a high risk of having the information used against you. This is why the TAB Board members on each board own businesses that are not in competition with each other; they are peers whom members can trust.

Many business owners have a relative or friend in the business world with whom they periodically bounce off ideas, but it is rare for mentors or friends to bring accountability to a Personal Plan or course change. Equally, it is very difficult to be totally open with a mentor, relative, or friend who knows your family well. Choosing to confide in someone who is too close to your personal life has the potential to create an uncomfortable situation.

One business owner confided in what he thought was a trusted friend about his dislike for his business partner and the stress level involved in dealing with the partner. The friend shared this confidence with his wife who in turn told the wife of the business owner's partner about the conversation. Family and friends cannot always be trusted to keep things confidential.

Obtaining review accountability in a structured manner each month from family and friends is not advisable—even from spouses who are working in the business with you. In the same way that entrepreneurs have elements of their written Statements that they do not want to share with employees, it is just as common for there to be elements they do not share with their spouse or relatives or friends.

Thousands of business owners look to their fellow TAB Board members to help them review, challenge, and revise their plans.

They use their fellow TAB Board members to be their sounding board and to help keep them accountable for their plans. TAB Board members understand the dynamics of life as a business owner. They are peers you respect so you can benefit from their welcome advice. They are there to share the challenges and problems, but they are also there to share the joy.

One way that TAB facilitator-coaches help to keep their members accountable is by asking each member, "What specific actions have you committed to completing prior to next month's meeting?" It is expected by all on the board that each member will report the status of these commitments at the next month's meeting.

Monthly coaching is another tool for bringing about review accountability. You are hundreds of times more likely to be successful in achieving your dreams if you have an impartial coach, like a TAB Board facilitator-coach, who is trained to help you through the process. Even Tiger Woods has admitted he needs a coach. It was more than a coincidence that after years of incredible success in winning major tournaments, he had a cold period after dropping his coach. If Tiger Woods can benefit from a coach to help him in a field in which he was the best, ask yourself whether a coach can help you overcome the roadblock of lack of personal accountability.

This is one of the reasons why TAB facilitator-coaches meet monthly with their TAB members. A TAB coach will not tell you what to do but rather will facilitate your decisions and nurture you when changes need to take place. Meeting with a TAB Board facilitator-coach for an hour or so each month will help keep you accountable for the changes needed to make your plans, including course changes, happen.

TAB membership includes monthly coaching sessions with the TAB-trained facilitator-coach who facilitates your TAB Board. TAB coaches are trained to understand the integrated nature of the personal and business lives of business owners and to help bring accountability to them. In addition to helping you focus on

keeping your commitments to your plans and course changes, a
TAB facilitator-coach will challenge you to schedule time to
monitor your results and help you review and modify your Personal Plan Statements as needed. They can often recognize—
when you are unable to—that you are going in a wrong direction
and can help get you back on course.

The process of running your life and business in an integrated
manner is not always an upward spiral. It is easy to get discour-
aged during backslides—and there will be backslides. Your fellow
TAB members and TAB facilitator-coach can help you with the
accountability you need to prepare for, and deal with, inevitable
backslides.

Changing Course Checklist

- Has something significant happened in your life to cause you
  to revise your Personal Vision Statement?
- Challenge the accuracy of your SWOT Statements, and
  make any needed changes. Make sure to look at factors such
  family, health issues, additions to your family, or changed
  economic needs.
- What factors have changed that may create a need to change
  your Personal Plan Statements (Critical Success Factors,
  Goals, Strategies, and Action Plans)?
- Do you have any Personal Plans that should be eliminated?
- Are you ready to add additional Personal Plans?
- Set aside a time each month to review your Vision
  Statement and SWOT Statements and each week to review
  your Personal Plans.
- Look for roadblocks that may thwart your course changes
  including:
  ○ Being unable to admit your mistakes

- ○ Employees, family members, or friends who resist your course changes
- ○ Chronic procrastination or taking too long to make course changes
- ○ A fear of making bold moves
- ○ Not knowing what you don't know
- ○ Lack of personal accountability

CONCLUSION

Moving from Ambition to Real Achievement

There is a story about a hurricane that brought with it severe flooding. When the water level started rising dangerously high, rescue boats were sent out. When one of the rescue boats went to Jim McDonald's house, the crew found Jim sitting on his roof. The men running the rescue boat yelled up to Jim to get into the boat.

Jim yelled back, "No. I will wait here. The water won't reach the roof because I am a believer, and God won't let me down."

Jim drowned.

Upon arriving at the Pearly Gates, Jim saw Saint Peter and cried out, "Why didn't God help me?"

Saint Peter responded, "Did you expect God to push you into the boat?"

Jim had his opportunity—he just didn't take it. Using the Seven Secrets of Great Entrepreneurial Masters is your opportunity to get what you want from life and work. The Seven Secrets show you what you need to do to become a winner. Using the Seven Secrets makes you hundreds of times more likely to be successful in achieving your dreams.

Adding Great Value to Your Life by Using Each of the Seven Secrets

An old adage calls ambition "the ingredient that makes the dough rise." But ambition is rarely enough to bring you the full happiness and success you desire. Making *any one* of the Seven Secrets a part of your day-to-day life will bring added value to your life. Integrating *all* Seven Secrets into your life creates a synergy through which the benefits increase exponentially.

Using the Secret of A Personal Vision will result in developing a written, long-range Personal Vision of what you want out of life that will be both the foundation you set and the target for which you reach. Remember Bill Courtney, the custom-home business owner who met with his family in order to incorporate the dreams his children had for their future involvement with the company with his own dreams? Without the knowledge he gained of his children's dreams, Courtney had no way to know if selling his business should be a part of his Personal Vision Statement. Upon completing his Personal Vision Statement and successfully setting his Personal Plans into action, Courtney told me, "For the first time in 17 years my family and business are 'rowing their oars' in the same direction."

You will use the Secret of A Look in the Mirror to identify your Strengths, Weaknesses, Opportunities, and Threats (SWOT) and understand how to make these elements the framework for developing Personal Plans that will allow you to achieve your dreams.

You will chart the course that leads the way to your dreams using the Secret of The Personal Plan by creating written Personal Plans that include the factors critical to your success, setting Goals to satisfy those Critical Success Factors, creating Strategies to achieve the Goals and making the Action Plans to make your Strategies successful.

Using the Secret of Results-Driven Communications to Make It Happen, you will assertively make your plans happen by using the six methods of building trusting two-way communications and the five tools to make your communications more successful and by learning how to smash through the four communications barriers that keep most business owners from getting what they want.

Not all of your Personal Plans will require negotiating skills to get results, but the seven guidelines to prepare for the negotiations and the ten techniques to use during the actual negotiations that are found in the Secret of Negotiating to Make It Happen will make many of your plans happen that would otherwise have gone nowhere.

The Secret of Creativity to Make It Happen will make your time management so effective that you will then have the needed energy to apply the creativity-producing techniques explained in this Secret to boost your creative abilities in order to make your Personal Plans happen.

Finally, you will use the Secret of Changing Course to review and revise your Personal Vision Statement, SWOT Statements, and Personal Plans and to identify and overcome the roadblocks that can keep you from making successful course changes.

By using the Seven Secrets of Great Entrepreneurial Masters, you will have a clear definition of what true fulfillment from your personal life and your work life means to you—your Personal Vision of Success—and be able to turn that vision into a reality. You will be able to merge and integrate your personal life and your work life to create the fulfilling life you desire.

Making Your Own Luck

When Branch Rickey, one of baseball's all-time great general managers, was told how lucky his teams were to have been so successful, he responded, "Luck is the residue of design." Certainly there is luck involved in such things as being born with aptitudes that allow you to do some things better than others, luck in having good health, and luck in being born into a family that provides positive nurturing. But even people who have been "blessed" with this sort of luck don't always succeed.

It is no coincidence that so many GEMs become "lucky" in business and in life. GEMs never fall back on "bad luck" as an excuse. They use the Seven Secrets to create the luck of their own design. You are much more likely to be lucky in achieving your visions and dreams and to become a winner if you make the Seven Secrets of GEMs part of your life.

Being Accountable to Yourself

The Seven Secrets provide the framework for reaching your dreams. But merely learning them is not enough. You must take the responsibility of integrating them into your life and your business and making them a part of your day-to-day life. You are the most important catalyst for the success—or failure—of your life and your company. As a business owner, your life is different from those who are employed by others. You control what you do, whom you do it with, when you do it, and, to a large degree, how much you earn. Managing the integration of your life and business is far more than a once-in-a-while activity. It is often the difference between a happy and fulfilled life and a life that is severely lacking in or devoid of these important factors.

Personal accountability is never easy, and there are always plenty of readily available excuses for avoiding it. This is not unlike the accountability needed to write a certain number of pages a day in order to write a book. I personally know how much personal accountability that takes! Usually there is no one else to hold you responsible for sticking with your Action Plans other than yourself.

Regularly meeting with other business owners is one way of providing the external source of accountability that many people need to reach their desired success. TAB Board members share their written Statements with their fellow TAB Board members and help to keep each other on track toward their dreams. Because members trust each other with all aspects of their visions and plans, including those items they keep Pocketed from others, the advice from within the TAB Board helps members stay focused in the right direction. Meeting with a trusted advisor, such as a TAB Board facilitator-coach, also helps keep you accountable for your Personal Plans.

Too many underachievers believe that success is an accident brought on by fate. They do not believe that they are in control of their own destiny. GEMs know that true success relies on how they manage themselves and the extent to which they take the full responsibility for doing this.

Applying the Seven Secrets Every Day

At a very early age my father taught me that in order to succeed you need patience and persistence. He believed that those who fail in business commonly view their race to success as a sprint and that those who view that race as a marathon are the ones more likely to win. He pointed out that those people who go into business with get-rich-quick ideas are typically the ones who fail. In contrast, those who succeed are usually the ones who clearly thought through what they wanted, had a plan to achieve it, and worked hard at making it happen.

The Seven Secrets should become a part of your belief structure so that you automatically use them whenever you are making important personal or business-related decisions. To make the most effective use of the Seven Secrets, you need to practice them by applying them every day. After Tipton was sold, I took time away from business for a few years. After I returned to the business world, I found that many of my skills that involved the Seven Secrets had become rusty and that I was responding to situations less sharply than in the past. It took practice to bring my skills in using the Seven Secrets back to their previous level.

Applying the Seven Secrets in All Areas of Your Life

Using the Seven Secrets is like putting money in the bank. The Seven Secrets first help you figure out what your dreams are and then help you combine your life and your work so that they meet those dreams. By charting a personal course to your success and happiness, the Seven Secrets allow you to prosper while enjoying the fruits of your labor.

You do not need to be a business owner to benefit from using the Seven Secrets. They will help anyone who wants to find greater personal happiness and work success. All of the principles expressed in the Seven Secrets that do not specifically deal with the uniqueness of business ownership will work just as well for nonbusiness owners. This is particularly true of those at the management level of their company's operations.

Most of us are faced with so many pressures that using the Seven Secrets for running our lives and leading our businesses is essential in maximizing success and enjoying life. The Seven Secrets are a tested and proven approach to life and business. They show you how to connect what's going on in your personal life with what's happening at work and how to merge your personal and work goals so your life is more enjoyable.

Realizing Your Personal and Business Visions of Happiness and Success

It is my sincere hope that you find the Seven Secrets shared within these pages helpful and that they lead you to realizing your personal and business visions of happiness and success. I feel passionate about these Seven Secrets that brought my—and so many others'—dreams to life.

The French poet and critic Guillaume Appolinaire wrote:

"Come to the edge," he said.
"We are afraid," they said.
"Come to the edge," he said.
They came; he pushed them, and they flew.

I know many of you feel a certain fear of taking the bold step needed to commit to this process. Come to the edge of your comfort zone with me, and fly to your dreams using the Seven Secrets of Great Entrepreneurial Masters as your wings.

Enjoy the journey!

Allen Fishman

Index

About the Author

Allen E. Fishman is the founder and CEO of The Alternative Board (TAB), the world's largest business peer board and coaching franchise system. He has been featured in a variety of media venues, including CNBC, Bloomberg, *The Wall Street Journal*, and *USA Today*. Fishman speaks at engagements around the world.